Christiana Tsai

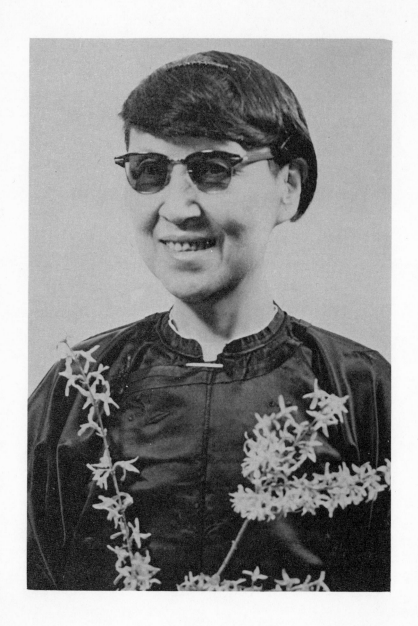

Christiana Tsai

by
Christiana Tsai

Pictures by James N. Howard

MOODY PRESS
CHICAGO

Library of Congress Cataloging in Publication Data

Tsai, Christiana.
    Christiana Tsai.

    1. Tsai, Christiana.   2. Christian biography—
China.   3. Christian biography—Pennsylvania—
Paradise.   4. Paradise, Pa.—Biography.
5. Malaria—Biography. I. Title.
BR1725.T69A33   248′.246   77-25085
ISBN 0-8024-1422-2

Printed in the United States of America

In Memoriam

Of my loving Godmother, Miss Mary A. Leaman, who led
me to the road of peace in Jesus Christ, our Saviour,
along which path we walked together for fifty-eight years,
and without whose help and prayers God's work through
me could never have been done.

Contents

Foreword

This is one of the most fascinating and challenging autobiographies I have ever read. It is the life story of a Chinese lady of distinction, a devout Buddist whose father was governor general during the late Manchu dynasty of the province of Kiang-su, where my parents later served as medical missionaries and where I was born and raised.

Christiana Tsai tells how she came to trust, love, and serve the living God through His Son, and how she was used, despite a lifetime of incredible suffering, to win thousands to Him.

I had the privilege of reading *The Queen of the Dark Chamber* and later meeting this living legend in her dark room, aware of an unseen Presence with us there.

It is that Presence—the Lord Jesus Himself—that this book is all about; how He in His wisdom and love selects some He can trust with an unusual ministry.

To Christiana Tsai He entrusted the ministry of serving Him with a bed for a pulpit, a darkened room for a workshop, years of incredible suffering as her constant companion, and hundreds of people won to the Lord Jesus as her reward.

Read it and worship Him!

RUTH BELL GRAHAM

THE GROWING DARKNESS CLOSES IN
Ruth Bell Graham

The growing darkness closes in
like some thick fog,
engulfing me—
a creeping horror—
'till I learned,
"The darkness hideth not from Thee."

"The earth was without form
and void."
Upon the deep
such darkness lay:
O Light, Who first created light,
do Thou the same
today!

As in a darkened room
one knows—
knows without sight—
another there,
so, in the darkness,
sure I knew
Thy presence
and the cold despair,
formless and chaotic, merged
to a soft glory;
As a child
terrified by dark,

lies quiet
within his mother's arms,
no wild
fears shall torment
my weakness now,
The dark—the dark—
surrounds me still.
But so dost Thou!

The future is a blank without a view.
That which I wanted most, You have denied;
I cannot understand (and I have tried);
There's nothing I can do but wait on You.

Earth offered much, and I had, lingered long
outside her lighted windows, wistful grown—
till at my side I heard a voice—Your own.
Lord, how could I resist a love so strong?

Take all away. I am content to know
such love is mine—for life is all too brief
to grieve for pleasures bringing only grief;
give me but You; it is enough just so.

Enough—and more! Such love in You keeps growing—
in You I find my deepest joy complete,
all longing satisfied, and pain made sweet;
in You my cup is filled to overflowing.

From *Sitting By My Laughing Fire,* by Ruth Bell Graham, Copyright 1977, Ruth Bell Graham, Word Books. Used by permission of Word Books, Publisher, Waco, Texas.

Preface

When I wrote my first book, *Queen of the Dark Chamber,* published in 1953, I was able to spend a year in comparative quiet concentrating on nothing else. I weighed and prayed over every line. After the book was published, a flood of visitors poured into our home: military officers from Taiwan, Chinese seamen, students, internationals, American women's missionary societies, church groups, and Sunday school children.

Jesus Christ, my Saviour and Lord, has continued to be the light of my dark chamber, the dimly lit bedroom in which I have spent more than forty-seven years. What has happened since I arrived in America in 1949 has been a continuing drama directed by the Lord. The reasons I am bedridden in a dark room and what has happened there and beyond is my story.

May God receive all the glory for what He has done in my dark chamber. My unceasing prayer is that He will always keep me humble. If the day ever comes when I am more interested in exalting myself than in exalting my adorable Lord Jesus Christ, God will surely put me aside. He has said, "My glory will I not give to another" (Isaiah 42:8).

It has been my privilege through the years to have met many friends in the Lord. They have contributed most helpful thoughts and advice to enable me to finish this sequel. It would not be fair to acknowledge one and omit others, so I want to express deep thanks and appreciation to all those who had a share.

Christiana Tsai

Acknowledgements

I praise the Lord for Christian friends who have helped me write this book, which is truly a cooperative effort. Initially, I was helped by Ellen L. Drummond, an old friend from China, who helped me to write *Queen of the Dark Chamber*.

Later I received the able assistance of Leona Choy, who spent many hours piecing together material out of my various speeches to visiting groups, as well as information growing out of our discussions, into a unified manuscript.

I am also grateful for the help of Jerry Jenkins, managing editor of *Moody Monthly*, who prepared the final draft.

Finally I would like to recognize the generous help of my three co-workers, Susanna Eshleman, Grace Ng, and Frances Stoltzfus, who have been with me more than twenty years.

Introduction

My job was simply to shape up an existing manuscript, edit and rewrite as necessary. It probably could have been done without my meeting the queen, Christiana, but what a privilege missed!

Moody Press thought it would give me added insight and a feel for the woman and her dark chamber. I wasn't quite sure what to expect. How bizarre, to think of a tiny Chinese woman, born into wealth in 1890, only to become a Christian at a girls' mission school, strike a lifelong friendship with the principal, serve the cause of Christ with her friend until they were forty and fifty years old, respectively, traveling throughout China and the United States, speaking, and writing.

And when a ravaging, mysterious illness (which took sixteen years to diagnose) relegated Christiana to bed in a dark room in 1931, it affected neither hers nor her friend China Mary's ministries, nor their friendship, which lasted until Mary's death in 1972.

So here was a woman who had fled China for the United States in 1949, the year I was born. She was sixty then and had already been bedridden for nearly two decades. Four years later her book, *Queen of the Dark Chamber,* would be printed for the first of thirty-six times by Moody Press, enjoying a worldwide readership in dozens of languages.

Did the queen truly have material for another book, or would there be too little to write about after being in bed so long? Could the last twenty-four or so years be as exciting and interesting as growing up in China, converting from Buddhism, and enjoying a fruitful, mobile ministry?

As it turns out, of course, the story of a woman who continues to engage in outreach, even from her darkened chamber in Pennsylvania, is a mind-boggler. From this little room in the huge old house emanates prayer, letter writing, and personal witnessing unparalleled by most who can walk.

The old Leaman home, left to Christiana by her lifelong friend, Mary (the last of the Leaman sisters), is a gigantic structure in Paradise, Pennsylvania. Christiana's small room is on one end of the house, right off the dining room. As you enter you see a Chinese light fixture which brightly illuminates one end of the room. A black kerchief blocks the light from Christiana's view. The shades are pulled. Two other small lamps are similarly draped to allow light on one end of the chamber, keeping the other end almost totally dark.

The little woman in the bed sits regally with back straight, shoulders square. Even in her dark chamber she wears the blackest sunglasses, old-fashioned with perfectly round lenses. The colorful Chinese lamp is a stark contrast to the dark bedspread, Christiana's black jacket, and the dim light. Her face is almost always brightened by a smile, and when she lifts her glasses to read with a magnifying glass, her smooth, full face evidences a soft beauty she has always called "plain."

She claims to be nervous about meeting yet another guest, though she has entertained hundreds and hundreds. And she works hard at breaking down the barrier caused by the strange scene of the Chinese queen in the big bed in the dark room in the big house.

To a stranger who knew nothing about this saint, the entire atmosphere could be frightening. It's a trip into the past. The rest of the house is filled with antiques, many much more than two hundred years old. The food is prepared from recipes that are either early Chinese or very early American. A guest is treated like a weary traveler and is made the center of attention—from a bowl and a pitcher of water (along with fruit and a box of crackers) waiting in his room, to Susanna and Grace (two helpers Christiana calls her co-workers) bustling in the kitchen and making sure he eats all he wants and takes more than he can eat.

Susanna is a quiet, matronly, at-ease American woman who calmly and quickly goes about her chores. Grace is a delightful Chinese woman who is constantly checking to make sure everything is just right.

Nothing in the house is new. It seems as if the world whizzes by outside this old home, and you leave not caring if you ever catch up with it again.

And the memory of the queen and the dark chamber is not of the darkness but of the queen and her Lord.

JERRY JENKINS

I would hide behind my nurse's apron and peek out at
people.

ONE

Bird of Paradise

The news spread like a prairie fire throughout the Pennsylvania countryside. "Miss Leaman brought back a Chinese to live with her!"

Indeed, when I came from the great, flowery kingdom of China to live in Paradise, Pennsylvania, I felt as if I were on display like the turkey I had bought in Shanghai many years before. Turkeys were rare in China. I heard that for some strange reason Americans were fond of eating them when they celebrated their Thanksgiving festival. I went to great lengths to purchase one as a special gift for my dear missionary friends, the Leaman family. I dragged my precious cargo in a cage on the train to Nanking. Fellow passengers nearly overwhelmed me to see and touch the strange bird. "What does it eat?" I was embarrassed to admit that I had no idea. Unfortunately, someone fed it malted milk, and it died before it could be properly prepared for the Leamans' extravagant dinner!

I became the strange bird of Paradise in my comfortable bedroom in the ancestral Leaman home. It was through the kindness and generosity of my lifelong friend and missionary co-laborer, Miss Mary Leaman, that I had arrived. Having been bedridden for nineteen years already, I could not escape. I learned how my American missionary friends must have felt when we had gone together on evangelistic trips to the China countryside. People were inquisitive about their white skin, blue eyes, and golden hair. Because I was often the only Chinese accompanying them, village women would unceremoniously push aside my dress to examine my skin to see if it were really the same color as their own. "Are you pure Chinese?" they would ask.

I dearly loved my new friends in America, but we had a lot to learn about each other and from each other. They would shyly file into my room to see the "Chinese girl," who was already nearly sixty years old! They were often ill at ease and at a loss to start a conversation. Finally came the inevitable question: "What do Chinese eat?"

I tried to be both polite and accurate. My childhood had been luxurious, with dozens of servants bowing and waiting on us to attend to our every wish. "In my province in the morning we had steaming bowls of soft rice porridge, biscuits, cold fish, and several vegetables. At noon we had soup, three vegetables, three meats, and rice. At 4 P.M., we always had tea and fancy cakes. Between meals we had many kinds of fruit and nuts. For dinner—"

Before I could add a detailed description of our main meal with its countless varieties and delicacies from far and near, eyes were wide in astonishment. "Oh! We thought Chinese were poor, ate only rice, lived in huts, had long fingernails, queues, and bound feet!"

Yes, America was to be a far different life than the one to which I was born behind the imperial walls of a wealthy home in China during the last days of the Manchu Dynasty. In His mercy, God did not permit me to see from the beginning that I would spend more than half of my lifetime as if in a goldfish bowl, continually on exhibition and seldom alone. I was to be helpless to the extent that others would have to attend to all my needs. From my childhood, such exposure and lack of privacy had been my worst dislike and deepest fear.

During my youth in China, the favorite sport of my many brothers was to tease their "plain" sister. They laughed at me because I was so different from my twenty-three other brothers and sisters. Most of them favored either the handsomeness of my father or the beauty of my mother, who was so charming that her relatives all called her the "Peking Beauty." "You are not our sister!" they taunted me. "You must have been born in a hut!"

This made me unbearably shy and sensitive. I would run to my nursemaid and sob, "Why didn't I get just a little of my mother's beauty?" I became afraid of strangers. I was such an introvert that in the excitement and bustling crowds of public occasions like the dragon festival, I would hide behind my nurse's apron and peek out at people. My throat seemed locked when I had to eat in front of people.

Chinese daughters of the wealthy studied within the family courtyards under the same tutors as their brothers until the age of ten. Then they were separated with lady tutors for the feminine arts. This gave me some relief from my brothers' harassment, but it resumed each time we gathered for New Year celebrations at the big pavilion in our garden.

There, out of earshot of our parents, we all did what we chose. Our father, understandably, disliked having his solitude disturbed by the boisterous ways of his two dozen children. We were allowed eighteen wonderful days to celebrate the new year, act out our own dramas, feast to our hearts' content, consume all manner of Chinese New Year goodies, gamble, and play our musical instruments. My brothers would run around me, clanging cymbals in my face and jeering, "See, see, your face is flat and shiny like the cymbals!" They pointed at a pan of water. "Round as a basin, too!"

I fussed and lamented before my mirror, trying to create a hair style to cover more of my face. I became obsessed with the desire to be alone.

As I grew older, I majored in classic Chinese. I loved to write Chinese characters. With brush in hand, I forgot all else. I devoured every book I could lay my hands on. "Books are much better friends than people!" I rationalized. They opened the doors of the outside world to me.

I had just three desires. Surely, I thought, they were not too much to ask of life. When I dreamed of the future, my wishes focused on a quiet life-style.

First, I felt I would be content if I had a fine study with an elegant desk, a comfortable chair, a good light, and solitude for open-ended reading and writing. But more than half of my life has been spent lying and sitting in a bed, unable to take care of my simplest needs. My blankets are my desk. Because my illness impaired my vision, I must use a magnifying glass, and I can read very little and with difficulty. The lamps and windows are covered with dark cloth to shield my light-sensitive eyes. For nearly fifty years I have been the "Queen of the Dark Chamber."

The second of my life desires was to have a handsome piano, not for performance but for expressing the melodies that surged in my heart since my conversion from Buddhism to Christianity. Jesus Christ brought joy and harmony to my life. I became proficient in playing the seven-stringed Chinese instrument, Tsih-Hsien-Ching, and studied piano under Western teachers. But for nearly a half century my infirmity has prevented me from touching any instrument or hearing loud noises. Sounds that others scarcely hear pierce my eardrums like a thousand gongs. The unceasing roar of heavy trucks on the highway outside my bedroom window thunders like a waterfall. When I first came to America, many a night I awoke taut with pain to find my fingers wedged inside my ears, thinking fretfully, *If they have to drive so fast, why can't they do it quietly and in the daytime?* When I am weak with my recurring malaria attacks, I seem to hear hundreds of spinning wheels whirring in my head.

My third desire was to possess a fine library of books and files, neatly organized and available for my every taste and convenience. My dearly treasured Chinese classics and Western favorites were lost as a result of my escape from China and much traveling. My few remaining important books, letters, and files are tied with identifying ribbons under my bed and stuffed in cheap cardboard boxes. Properly brought up and fastidious, I would never have allowed anything to be stored under my bed in my early years! Now I must bend over and search under my bed for what I want, or forever trouble others to do so.

I had other simple desires—to stroll in cool forests, run in fields, wade in sparkling streams, climb mountains, and explore countries I had read about while behind my courtyard walls. When I first became ill, before my fortieth year and in the prime of my active life and service for the Lord, my doctor had warned, "You might even be in bed as long as three weeks!" I had sobbed uncontrollably.

"How can I endure such a long illness? Nearly a month!" It now has been nearly half a century.

Is God cruel because He has withheld almost all my early desires? No! "No good thing will he withhold from them that walk uprightly" (Psalm 84:11). Do I call the Lord unjust? No! "Shall the clay say to him that fashioneth it, What makest thou?" (Isaiah 45:9). Throughout my many years of illness, I have never, never, never dared to ask God why He allowed me to suffer for so long. I only ask Him what He wants me to do. With the apostle Paul, I testify, "For I have learned, in whatsoever state I am, therewith to be content" (Philippians 4:11). I believe that all that has happened to me was God's best choice for me. It has been far more satisfying than my three desires. I have no disappointment in His appointment.

When I finished *Queen of the Dark Chamber* in 1953, I thought certainly that my life's story was completed. Surely the next page would contain the longed-for words, "The End." Then I would be lifted out of my dark chamber to triumphantly greet my King of light, Jesus Christ, face to face in heaven. The poem that I quoted on the last page of my book was "The Rest of the Way," because I doubted that there was really much left for me.

My Lord planned otherwise. There was a sequel about to take place with a new setting: Paradise, Pennsylvania.

Often in my weakness I do not even know what lines to speak to meet the deep spiritual needs of those whom God has brought from all over the world to this out-of-the-way place. But over and over again, the Holy Spirit has been the never failing Prompter who supplies the lines and speaks through this weak channel. Jesus Christ, the light of my dark chamber and the light of the world, continues to shine brilliantly into the hearts of men and women as they have come to my bedside through the years. All the glory belongs to Him.

TWO

Raised in Luxury

To awaken to a chorus of birds outside the latticework of my window in Nanking, China, was a childhood delight. Our nurses would prop up the youngest group of my twenty-three brothers and sisters like a row of hungry swallows. They tucked our gaily colored silken quilts around us and brought in boxes of delicious English cookies. Some were shaped like fans, others like vases and butterflies; they had been given to Father by British businessmen who sought his political or economic favor.

We did not fully realize how noted Father was until gradually we observed the homage and respect paid him. He came from an old Confucian family that for generations had produced scholars who took China's ancient civil service examinations. Father held a number of important offices under the Manchu Dynasty, among them the governorship of Kiangsu Province. We children were born in the lap of luxury, prosperity, and fame. But within we were spiritually dark.

We were more impressed with the gifts lavished upon Father by business associates than with his position. He received cases of imported soda pop, a rare and expensive product in those days. But no one dared drink this foreign potion—who knew but that one might turn into a foreign devil? Our servants were instructed to pour the contents down the gutters and reuse the bottles for soy sauce and sesame oil. Far more elaborate gifts, which I now wish we had appreciated, were beautiful, shiny coal-burning stoves, complete with pipes and connections. Literally dozens of these expensive items were given to us, and the servants just stored them in a corner of our garden. We played our imaginative games around them while they became weather-beaten and rusted.

We certainly did not enjoy any pal relationship as children do with their "daddies" in the Western world. We stood in awe of Father, bowing to him in reverence. We were allowed to eat with him only at New Year's.

One of our favorite events was the dragon procession with its many floats. All the officials sat on a big reviewing stand. Father would be dressed in a splendid gown. (Particular costumes were worn only at certain celebrations each year and then carefully put away.) For this event, trays heaped with silver medals were stacked before him on the platform. He as governor awarded the performers.

Our excitement mounted as the sound of drums, cymbals, and many other instuments approached from a distance. A long silk dragon, maneuvered from the inside by soldiers, would writhe and wind and leap around, eventually dividing and forming four Chinese characters: *Tien Hsia Tai Ping,* meaning "world peace." Skyrockets and fireworks, which we watched from the garden at night, were set off for the occasion. I was always afraid of such commotion and hung close to my nurse.

Father was not a Christian but was friendly to the foreigners. As acting governor when the antiforeign Boxer Rebellion broke out in 1900, he received the Empress Dowager's edict ordering him to kill all foreigners. At the risk of his own life, he altered the documents to read "protect" instead of "kill" all foreigners, saving the lives of Westerners in our province. As things turned out, the empress never learned of this change, for she herself soon had to flee from an allied army that marched on Peking to release foreigners inside the besieged city.

As children, we were not much aware of the world beyond our high walls. We lived in spacious separate apartments. When my brothers married, they and their brides moved into their own apartments with us. Eventually there were about one hundred people within our walls. We would not have dreamed of mingling with those of lower rank.

But isolation did not insulate us from sin. We knew the difference between right and wrong. We often deliberately did wrong. I remember as a child sneaking nuts, lichees, and sweets right off the supposedly sacred altars of our ancestors at Chinese New Year. We children took turns being on watch while the transgressions went on.

I was closer to my nurse than to my mother, and sometimes while Mother was occupied gambling, I would steal candles from her apartment and give them to my nurse, who sent them to her home in the country. Piled in a certain cupboard were strings of one hundred Chinese coins. Time and again I stole a string of cash for my nurse.

Most of my family were addicted to opium smoking. It began when Western powers seeking to trade with China insisted on paying for fragrant Chinese tea with Indian opium. The Chinese government justifiably resisted such immoral enslavement of its people, but Chinese merchants were not so conscientious.

Each member of our family was given his or her own beautiful silver-engraved pipe, which the servants kept clean and polished for his drug habit. When opium is smoked, pain goes, strength decreases, and a lazy, withdrawn feeling sets in. Appetite is diminished. (I often heard the warning that China would surely be overrun and divided by her enemies because opium smokers would not have the motivation to resist.)

Seeing the rest of my family indulge, and being aware of the negative results, I resisted opium even before I became a Christian. I often had stomach pains, but I determined that I would not smoke opium to get relief. Once when the pain was particularly bad, I was persuaded to take just a little ball of it. The relief was so instant and pleasurable that it scared me. I was strongly tempted to continue, but when the pain came back, I refused to become a servant to any drug. I would rather die.

I diligently practiced the prayers, burning of incense, and reading of Buddhist classics. Often one of my sisters-in-law and I went to worship in the Ling-yin Buddhist temple on a hill in Hangchow. A long flight of steps led to the top, and we tried to bow on every third step. I took Buddhism seriously, even having prepared to enter a convent. And I was very zealous to fulfill all religious requirements, but my physical endurance was small. We young girls, not seeing anyone around to check on us, waited until we nearly reached the top before we started our bowing!

Monks often came to our home to do sorcery. All our family believed in their powers. It was this belief in fortune-tellers that changed the course of my life regarding marriage.

When I was only a child, the year, month, day, and hour of my birth were matched with those of a boy child whose family was seeking a favorable arranged marriage for their son when we would both come of age. My statistics were interpreted as being either extremely good or extremely bad. His family decided not to take the risk! In His marvelous plan for the ages and for each of our lives, our heavenly

Father watches over even the superstitious actions of men, guarding us from misfortune until we come into His fold.

By the time I was sixteen, my spirit longed to fly away and learn new things in new places. I had long since exhausted the books and scrolls my tutors considered proper for females to study. A school for girls had been opened nearby by some missionaries named Leaman, and I gave my father no peace until he allowed me to study there. My nickname was "Too Many," based on the comment of my father at my birth. (His house was already overflowing with children!)

Even so, I was a faithful daughter and beloved of my parents. But my father did not consider his fondness for me reason enough to transgress the ancient tradition against advanced education for girl children. I continued to plead with him. Finally relenting, he warned, "But beware not to eat Christianity!"

"I promise, Father!" I cried happily.

THREE

"Eating" Christianity

It was in part the vision of American missionary Charles Leaman's wife, Lucy, that brought the Ming Deh Girls' School in Nanking into being. She realized the strategic potential of a Christian girls' school when as a young woman she served on the faculty of True Light Girls' School in south China. Girls in China rarely learned to read, nor were they interested in doing so. Mrs. Leaman advertised for months, with all manner of enticements to obtain pupils, but none responded. The first pupil had to be paid to study!

No one would have dared to dream that during the lifetime of the Leaman daughters the school would have an enrollment of sixteen hundred students. Ming Deh was the pioneer girls' school and forerunner of dozens of such schools right in Nanking.

You can imagine the commotion when I arrived at the school in 1906 in my fashionable clothes and sedan chair. "I want to register so I can learn to speak English and play the piano," I announced. I had an air of authority befitting my station in life, but it was so out of place in that peaceful mission compound.

That was when I met Miss Leaman, the daughter of Charles and Lucy Leaman. She was tall and thin, dressed in simple Chinese clothes. I was a sixteen-year-old girl. She

30

was the twenty-six-year-old principal. Her quiet manner and voice conveyed to me the inner beauty, peace, and strength that I had sought but missed all my young life. In the mysterious plan of God, Miss Leaman and I were destined to live and work together for the Lord for fifty-eight years.

Upon learning who I was, Miss Leaman dared not accept me as a boarder to share the "coarse food and household chores." I was to be a day student, but only if my mother would come in person to give permission for me to enroll. Although such action was beneath Mother's station and dignity, she reluctantly agreed and I was accepted.

Mingling with common girls in a classroom was a new life-style to me, but I was eager to break through to the outside world. I questioned my classmates during my first exposure to chapel service. I was bewildered. "You say we are worshiping, but I do not see any idols or gods. There is just a plain platform with a man speaking from it." I did not understand the strange theological vocabulary. My mind wandered. I started to chatter with the other girls, distracting them. Lucy Leaman quietly cornered me and explained that we were worshiping a God that we could not see. Often bored, I would slip a detective novel into my pocket to read during the sermon.

But that thirst for knowledge was the gateway to my salvation. Despite my lifelong training and the rash promise to my father, I began to attend a Bible class with the other girls, merely as another opportunity to improve my English. "I can quit anytime I want to," I reasoned.

Then one day in chapel I heard the famous American preacher S.D. Gordon speak about "Jesus, the light of the world." My spiritually blind, rebellious eyes were opened. I saw my sinful condition before the Lord and His provision for my salvation through the cross of Christ. I fled to my room and yielded my heart to Him. Peace and joy and light flooded my soul.

Though my father had already passed away, the rest of my Buddhist family threatened me, mocked me, and made me a prisoner in my own home. But my Lord never failed me. Eventually He answered my prayers to melt their hard hearts.

One day while strolling in my private garden, I thought of how peaceful and pleasant life was in the security of our palatial home. I was walking slowly up the steps to my private tower when my attention was drawn to the window. Was that smoke billowing up over the horizon of Nanking in the distance? My Bible lay open to Psalm 91:2: "He is my refuge and my fortress: my God; in him will I trust."

I had just committed this psalm to memory, but now its almost staggering promises seemed to leap out of the pages. Was God preparing me for something? My eyes followed the suspicious line of rapidly spreading smoke. It had turned from gray to an ominous black. Red flashes leaped into the sky behind it. My heart began to pound. Would Nanking be next in the unceasing fight between the warlords of China?

Many, including some members of our family, had already fled to the Shanghai Concession for safety. But several of my brothers and their families didn't want to leave our comfortable, luxurious mansion. My mother and I had also stayed, taking our chances, hoping that the worst would not happen. I looked over the treetops of my garden. A heavy, strange stillness hung in the air.

The bombardment of guns in the distance shook my glassed-in tower. My servant girl pounded on my door. "Seventh mistress, hurry! Soldiers are coming! The South City has fallen to the bad ones, and bullets are flying everywhere!" She fell to her knees. "They are looting *our*

"Soldiers are coming!"

street!"

I could hear the crack of rifle fire from the streets and nearby houses. A manservant ran up my stairs and his words tumbled out: "They are searching for the master and mistress of each house! They hang them and beat them, doing terrible things until they give them everything. You must flee!"

A third servant joined them, sobbing, "They are coming toward our house now! They ars shooting at our iron gates!"

My brothers and the rest of the family raced to a secret door of escape. What did it matter now how beautiful, ornate, or valuable our possessions were? Children screamed, women wailed, and the men tried to keep them quiet so the soldiers would not discover us.

FOUR

Brush with Death

I pulled my mother from her quarters as she struggled along on bound feet. She was not used to walking rapidly nor far, and in her panic she twisted her ankle. "Daughter, I can't go on—I'm hurt! I will only slow everyone down, and then all will be caught and murdered. Go on without me. I am old and useless—go!"

"No, Mother. I love you. You are precious to me—and to God!" I prayed under my breath, "O, dear Lord, I claim all those promises I have just been reading. Protect us all. You promised that 'it shall not come nigh thee.'* Dear Jesus! Save us from this destruction!"

The rest of the family had escaped over the wall, and I was left alone with Mother in my arms. She cringed with pain, and our dog, Proper, followed us, whimpering and barking. I commanded, "Proper, stay!" and he obeyed. Had he followed us, he might have revealed our hiding place. The rifle fire was getting closer. I heard swords clang against our iron gate and feet kicking the massive doors.

The Lord gave me sudden wisdom and unusual strength. Though slightly built, I hoisted Mother to my back and staggered toward the rear entrance to the servants' quarters. By now bullets were flying over our heads. Mother was in a near faint and like a dead weight. I could hear the soldiers

---
*Psalm 91:7b

laughing and ranting while the servants tried to appease them with our best food and wine.

I kicked open the servants' quarters back door and frantically looked for a dark place under the stairway. I tried to quiet my mother's sobbing so that we would not be discovered. I, who had always been so fastidious, unable to stand the least dirt or discomfort, found myself crouched beneath the stairs in wet muck. Years of accumulated spider webs hung from the musty beams, and spiders of all descriptions brushed against my hair and cheeks. I clapped my hand over my own mouth to keep from crying out. The moldy odor filled our lungs with the chill of a tomb. I sat in the mud and held my mother on my lap. "Mother, Mother," I whispered. "Jesus will help us. He promised!"

Though a new Christian, I realized that the Lord had placed me in a very responsible position as His witness. He would not forsake me. My teeth chattered as I prayed, "Lord, help me to be a good testimony for You. I am no use dead!"

Having had their fill of wine, the soldiers grew bolder in their search for the rest of the family and their treasures. They demanded that the servants reveal the hiding places. Several staggered across to the servants quarters in the very courtyard where we hid. Mercifully, my mother had fallen into a dazed stupor and was not aware of our brush with death. As the heavy footsteps came within inches of us, I held my breath and prayed more desperately, again pleading the promises from the precious psalm which God had given me that morning:

"For he shall give his angels charge over thee, to keep thee in all thy ways" (Psalm 91:11).

The heavy boots moved on. Although we were under the stairway for only a few hours, it seemed like an eternity.

When a siren pierced the air, my mother roused and cried out, not remembering where she was, and clinging to me with such fierceness that her fingernails dug into my arm. The soldiers cursed and stamped their feet, calling to one another gruffly that it was time to return to their barracks.

Before long, the noise of the firing faded into the distance, and silence settled over the whole courtyard. We remained huddled under the stairway until the servants resumed their normal work and tried to straighten out the chaos left by the soldiers.

Finally, I stretched my legs, numb from the dampness and cramped position. Mother's ankle was swollen to nearly twice its normal size, and she cried out as I tried to drag her into the light. I hoisted her to my back again, trembling with weakness. My legs felt like rubber as I staggered back over the winding paths to the main house.

My brothers and sisters also had crawled out of their hiding places after the siren had drawn away the soldiers. They were grief-stricken, supposing the worst, expecting to see Mother hanging mutilated by the soldiers. When they caught sight of me with her on my back, they ran crying and throwing themselves on the ground before us with relief and joy.

"It is God who has saved us," I whispered faintly. "Hurry and wipe the cobwebs from Mother's face, change her clothes, and soak her foot."

As I sat huddled in blankets with my servant trying to rub circulation back into my feet, my brothers came to question me further about my saying the Lord had delivered us. I sensed their embarrassment and said, "Brothers, it is the only, true, living God who can deliver us in trouble. Idols and incense are no use in the face of disaster. They cannot save us. They cannot give us peace." I saw an unusual

We were just part of a human mob desperately fighting to escape.

gentleness and the first flicker of faith in their eyes. I knew it would not be long before the Good Shepherd would bring more of my family into His fold.

Because of the continued danger and looting, we were advised to flee Nanking and go to Shanghai. "We will keep house for you," promised one faithful old servant and his wife. What to take and what to leave behind? Every refugee faces such painful decisions—that is, if he has enough time before his flight. He never knows whether he will ever return. Because my own treasure was in heaven, I did not face the heartbreaking decisions my family had to make.

As we began to leave, my brothers said, "Sister, you look too much like a wealthy person. You will be robbed and beaten for your valuables, whether you are carrying any or not. Why don't you disguise yourself?"

I borrowed my servant's rough jacket, padded trousers, and simple cloth shoes. "Oh, mistress, your face is too light and your hair too stylish," said my servant girl. While I fastened back my hair into a bun, she ran out for a pan of water in which she had soaked walnut shells. "Here, rub this solution on your face. It will make you look darker."

As we stepped outside our gates, it was as if we had fallen into a roaring sea of people who swept us along. Shouting, crying, pushing one another, we were all on an equal level. We were just part of a human mob desperately fighting to escape for our lives. Servants accompanied us, some struggling under heavy bundles of our valuables, others pushing wheelbarrows of provisions.

I said to one of my brothers, "You are strong; you go ahead of us and push. I will carry Mother again."

Arriving at the train platform, we pushed ourselves through the narrow door with hundreds of other frantic people. People were jammed together on the train with scarcely breathing space between them. Baggage filled the aisles, and the odor of human sweat hung heavy in the air.

"Please," I begged two women already squeezed into a single seat, "let my injured mother have a little corner of your seat. She can't stand up." In kindness and pity, they huddled still closer together, and I dropped my mother into a safe corner. Mother still had her bad opium habit and was in such pain that I was forced to give her pills at intervals.

Although I was disguised as a poor servant so that even my mother was startled, in my heart I was still rejoicing that I was the "child of a King"—Jesus was my Lord. It must have shown through. A gentleman came over to me, staring curiously. "Do you believe in Jesus?" he asked.

"Yes, I do!" I replied without hesitation. Mother looked at me, questioning, "Tell me, daughter, what kind of a sign did you make that a stranger would know that you belong to Jesus?" I just smiled.

FIVE

Miss Mary Leaman

Joy and relief overwhelmed us when we finally pulled to a jerking halt in the Shanghai station. "Hurry, hire rickshaws," ordered my brothers, and within minutes we were on our way to my fifth sister's house. Mother was still on my lap, and the servants were still piled high with baggage. It was nearly midnight when our servants knocked at the gate. We had had no way to notify my sister of our coming.

We had caught a glimpse of a newspaper when we alighted from the train. It declared in bold headlines that the city we had just left was burned to ashes, and all the people had been killed. Now from inside we could hear wailing and cries of mourning. The odor of incense floated to our nostrils on the damp night air. Then it dawned on us—it was probably for *us* they were mourning! They were burning paper money and other paper replicas so that we might have provisions for our journey into death!

The servant who came to open the gate turned white when she saw us. She ran away without opening the gate, and we were left shivering in the night, knocking.

My fifth sister was astonished when she saw us. She could not contain herself for joy! I committed Mother into her care; but because of their already crowded quarters, the rest of us had to search for a hotel where we could have a room.

41

When I finally entered a room in the wee hours of the morning, I collapsed on the floor.

Much later I was awakened by one of our family who had heard peddlers outside and bought me a bowl of dumpling soup. I ate it eagerly and fell back to sleep. In my semiconscious state, I could hear my family whispering.

"Wherever did Seventh Sister get such strength, wisdom, and courage to carry Mother like that?"

"It must have been her Jesus helping her."

I believe it was this incident that really planted the seed in Mother's heart, causing her to realize the love and power of Christ.

After we had returned home to Nanking, Mother tried to break her opium habit in a Quaker hospital. Miss Mary Leaman fasted and prayed for God's deliverance. At the end of two weeks of struggle, Mother suddenly seemed to be aware of a glow of unusual love as she gazed on Miss Leaman's face. She broke out with heavy perspiration, and at that moment the opium habit left her.

After she returned from the hospital, Mother announced to her children, "It was Jesus who answered the prayers of Miss Leaman and healed me." She urged, "My wish is that all my children and I will serve the living God." One of my brothers had believed secretly before her conversion, and through the years, fifty-five of my relatives accepted Christ. At this time I chose my English name, Christiana, after I was so moved by reading John Bunyan's book *Pilgrim's Progress*.

Mother was baptized at the church Charles Leaman had built, and seven of our family joined her. Mother was an intelligent but illiterate woman after the custom of women in China. She was taught by her grandson Woodrow to read from a picture book of the New Testament with big characters. In the summer, even neighbors joined us for prayers.

They marveled that Mother, who had been far from talkative before her conversion, now began to witness to them with great liberty.

One day Miss Leaman and I were in my prayer tower studying the Bible when Mother called to her. "Miss Leaman, I don't know how to express my gratitude to you for leading our family to find the true God through Jesus Christ. Would you accept my seventh daughter to be your daughter in the Lord?" From that time on, we accepted this beautiful spiritual relationship together and I called her Godmother.

Miss Leaman often bore much pain and suffering patiently and silently. As a result of a fall and injury to her spine when she was three years old, she found it hard to stand in the pulpit and address a crowd. Moreover, her gift from the Lord was a deep and quiet one. She was behind the scenes, in prayer, doing personal work and spiritual creative thinking. When traveling from place to place for meetings in China, she had to lie flat while being carried. So when we joined together to serve the Lord, He used her to prepare me for a public ministry which I had always shunned. She pushed me to the front and pulled me out of myself to allow the Lord to use me. "But Godmother, I don't want to," I often complained.

"Suppose you had a pen that refused to write. Would you stop writing?" she prodded me. "Of course not. You would change to another one. You can't change God's plan by refusing to do as He asks. He will change to another instrument, and you will lose your opportunity!"

When I was asked to speak at my commencement exercises, I was literally sick with fear. But the audience applauded every sentence, to my embarrassment. When it was over, they applauded so much, asking me to come out and bow again and again, I thought I would faint. A teacher had to prepare a special drink to revive me!

The mayor invited me to tea, and I was further embarrassed as he bowed to me, just a schoolgirl. He offered to arrange for me to speak to large audiences in cities throughout China on the importance of women's education. But I declined, saying that I was there to study.

When I graduated, many positions were offered me: to become vice-principal of my school, general secretary of the YWCA, and traveling lecturer to promote women's education. It was not that I was so much better than others, but that I was one of the first and very few Chinese girls to obtain a Western education. A Chinese proverb sums it up: "Where there are no big trees on the mountain, even the blades of grass are honored."

But the new King of my life had not called me to any of these honored positions, but to witness for Him. I traveled through most of the provinces of China, speaking and interpreting at various meetings and conferences. Many times it was in the company of such notables as Miss Ruth Paxson, Dr. Griffith Thomas, Dr. Charles Trumbull, and others.

It was a special joy for me to be a friend of the well-known speaker and writer Miss Paxson. I must have interpreted for her about three hundred times. She was known for speaking so rapidly in English that others could not keep up with her. But God gave us a oneness so that we seemed to think unitedly and deliver the messages with one spirit. I translated into Chinese her famous book, *Rivers of Living Water,* and also a compilation of her prayers and exhortations.

Thus God had begun to work through me.

SIX

Stricken

How I marvel at my naivety as a high-born, daintily raised girl! At Laura Haygood School every subject was taught in English by resident American teachers and by the wives of professors from a university. Miss Mary Culler White, a missionary-evangelist much used by the Lord in China, took some of us who were "more refined" girls along to conduct meetings on her houseboat. We knew little about taking care of ourselves, as we had always been waited on by servants. So we were totally ignorant of common daily chores. We just sat around with folded hands, while she, a missionary, cooked, cleaned, washed the dishes, and cleaned the commodes. She even ate from our plates like a servant after we had finished!

Often I prayed and worked with this dear missionary until after midnight, translating her messages into Chinese. I have always had the deepest respect for the missionaries who left their comfortable lands and homes for the sake of the gospel. Many sacrificed their very lives for Him and for my own countrymen.

Later I accepted a position as a music teacher in a Chinese government girls' school. Seventy-two of the two hundred students accepted Christ through opportunities I had to talk with them during intermissions. They often came to my home and to Bible classes in our church. The newspapers reviled me, calling me "the music teacher who is an evangelist, teaching the students to cry 'God, God!' and bringing anger from their parents." Indeed, many of my students did suffer persecution for their new faith in Christ and were faithful through great trials.

Because the missionaries with whom I traveled spoke mostly to Christians, I often held special services for non-Christians. We spoke to teachers and students of government schools in China, to mission colleges and high schools in many large cities, to nurses in hospitals, and to crowds of various sizes. When there was no building large enough to contain the crowds, tents were erected. In some of the student centers, I lived in the dormitories in order to be close to the students.

After speaking sometimes three times a day, I was busy until late at night with personal interviews. Besides the ministry in the cities, we traveled to the countryside and remote villages, living in primitive conditions. We traveled by railway, riverboats, coastal steamers, sedan chairs, wheelbarrows, houseboats, and rickshaws. We encountered many oppositions and trials, but the Lord was our vanguard to prepare the hearts of countless people in all walks of life to receive Him.

Rather than accepting other honored positions, I finally joined in serving the Lord with my dearest companion and co-worker, Miss Mary Leaman. God gave us deep love and harmony in this ministry together. I was able to continue living in my own home. If I had not, it would have been impossible for any Christian to enter our house, because the class distinction was so strong.

I teased Miss Leaman in later years that she had never actually invited me to join her. And when I did offer myself, all she quietly commented was, "May the Lord Jesus guide you." Time and again when I asked what she thought of my doing this or that, she did not commit herself but used this same reply. I must confess, it almost irritated me as a young believer. I said to myself, "Why doesn't she have that sentence printed? Every time she writes me she could just enclose a copy!"

But how right she was. In life's decisions we should get our directions straight from God. We may ask counsel from fellow believers and those with spiritual insight, but in the final analysis God must speak to our own hearts.

We lived and worked together, caring for one another through illnesses, civil wars, crises of life, and seemingly insurmountable problems. After I started working with Miss Leaman in Nanking, a storm of questions arose. The principal of Soochow school, Miss Ruth Paxson, and many other missionaries came, one by one, all with good intentions, to ask her why she kept me from working for the Lord nationwide. "Nanking is just one place," they argued.

But she certainly had not "kept me"! It was the Lord who intertwined our lives and destinies. But it showed again the wisdom she had in the way she always answered me— leaving the decision up to me.

Beginning in 1930 and continuing for seven years, Miss Leaman was to accomplish her greatest work. Her conviction was that the illiterate masses of China must have the Chinese Bible in some more simplified form than the complicated ancient Chinese written characters. This launched her into a monumental work. She transcribed and printed the Chinese Bible, putting the phonetic simplified characters in parallel columns beside the standard characters. The Chinese Nationalist government had already endorsed this phonetic system.

Miss Leaman was both completely unqualified and superbly qualified for this task. She operated on a shoestring budget, had a cubbyhole for an office, used volunteer proof-readers, and had only one expert printer-mechanic who cast the type matrices by hand. Already retired from her mission for physical disability, she was in constant pain and weakness, and her goal seemed impossible. She faced opposition and lack of sympathy even from unexpected sources. But she had a thorough knowledge of Chinese, an iron will, and a boundless faith that this was the job to which the Lord had called her. The phonetic Bible would not be off the press for more than thirty years.

One winter morning in 1931, I awakened with unbearable pain piercing my eyes, the room whirling, my head burning with fever, and my body stiffening. I lay more dead than alive, unable to eat, unable to move, for seventeen days. I couldn't speak more than a grunt for eight months and could not open my eyes for a year and a half. As I became more desperately sick, Miss Leaman had to lay aside her translation work and devote most of her daylight hours to nursing me. That left only her tired-out night hours for her proofreading.

Six doctors of different nationalities were called in for consultations. They all pronounced my case hopeless. A most famous Chinese doctor was asked to come and see me, and a large sum of money had to be paid in case he was kidnapped between his home and ours. He held my hand, saying, "You are like a lamp without oil. The longest you can live is three more days." My family prepared the coffin and grave clothes.

But Miss Leaman's prayers, faith, and courage kept me alive by God's power through this valley of the shadow of death, and through many more such valleys in the years to come.

In 1937, just as Miss Leaman had begun to make headway on her translating, the Japanese invaded China. But that did not stop her. After the Japanese attack on Pearl Harbor in 1941, she refused repatriation with other missionaries in order that she might complete her job. Because of that, she was imprisoned for two years in a Japanese concentration camp with other sick and crippled foreigners. I continued on my sickbed with malignant malaria of the bone marrow for the whole time she was in the camp.

On Christmas Eve of that year, much to everyone's amazement, I was still alive. One doctor publicly told her large atheistic family, "I have watched Miss Tsai's case so long that now I know there must be a God. My son and I have decided to believe in Jesus as our personal Saviour!" God wonderfully saved my old gateman, the head of those who guarded the main entrance, courtyards, and gardens of our home during the thirty-five years of my father's life as a government official. When he heard of my hopeless condition, he went to the pastor and said, "I want to go where my 'Miss Seven' goes." Thus, he was instructed in the faith and believed and was baptized a few months before he went to be with the Lord.

Once when I was near death I saw a vision of heaven and heard wonderful singing. I thought, *My time has come. What a welcome!*

But I seemed to hear a voice saying, "No, not a welcome, only a rehearsal!" My illness was not correctly diagnosed for sixteen long years of suffering, and by then it was too late for a cure. The malaria, with many related afflictions, laid me permanently aside from the physically active ministry I had before. My ear canals, that give balance, are all disconnected, so my equilibrium is destroyed. I cannot walk without reeling back and forth like a crab and falling if not supported. My eyes cannot bear direct light. I stay in a dark room with shades pulled, lights covered, and wear sunglasses.

One day in America an ear, nose, and throat specialist walked into my room and announced, "Miss Tsai, I know you are a refugee in this country. I am a specialist. You cannot afford to pay me. I want to give you a good examination to see why you cannot walk, just for curiosity."

He made the room dark and turned me in all kinds of directions. I was most thankful when he stopped. Then he said, pointing up to heaven, "Miss Tsai, only *that* Doctor can make you walk again. You will never walk in your life. You know, of course, that each ear has three canals that give balance. The canals in both your ears are all disconnected." He didn't know what had caused this. I begged him to operate, but he just said with a smile, "I repeat, only the Doctor in heaven can make you walk again."

SEVEN

Timekeeper

When we fled Shanghai one steaming day in August, we were trying to find some clothes for Miss Leaman to change into. "Why, there's nothing here but phonetic Bible materials!" I exclaimed as we rummaged through every one of Miss Leaman's suitcases. It was just like her—putting God's work before her comfort. She had ordered that none of her personal effects or clothes be packed, giving priority to the Bible materials she wanted to be kept safe. Our old servant, Pooh, loaned her something to wear.

In fact, we had not packed at all in the rush of leaving. Pooh had packed. And for some unknown reason, she had also packed a secondhand clock bought by Miss Leaman's father in Nanking years before. It was beautiful, kept good time, and had always been in the Leaman home. The servants just loved it, so they sneaked it along. The clock refused to tell time after its long, bumpy trip, but it did remind me that when Miss Leaman went into the concentration camp and I moved to my attic room, among our joint possessions was that broken clock.

One day a friend asked me to pray for a Chinese schoolteacher, his wife, and three children. They had barely enough to eat. "He repairs watches and clocks so he can buy food for his family," he said, asking me if there was any way we could help by letting people know about the availability of a repairer of clocks.

I told him that if the man would come to my home, I would give him our broken clock to repair. The friend said that the clock repairer was not able to come and get clocks, but I maintained that if he wanted the work, he would have to come and see me. Meanwhile, I spoke to some of my friends about his need and accumulated considerable work for him. I even offered to pay his rickshaw fare to my place.

Finally he came, with a very long face. Inviting him to sit down, I talked to him about salvation in Christ. He never answered one word. He wanted the job but was not eager to hear about Jesus. I kept back some of my friends' watches and did not give them to him all at once so that I could keep him coming. He took the Leaman clock to his home first.

Early one hot summer morning as I was being visited by a missionary, Mrs. Allison, who was waiting to go back to America, I heard bitter crying outside my screen door. I asked someone to go and see what the trouble was. A beautiful lady, as lovely as cherry blossoms after the rain, came shyly in.

"Miss Tsai, I am the clock man's wife," she said. "He is dying of tuberculosis. The blood just flows out, and there is no way to stop it. We have a tiny room with one bed for five of us. I have no money." When Mrs. Allison heard the story, she gave the equivalent of one or two American dollars to the lady. "I will tell my husband to go to see your husband," she promised.

When Mr. Allison called on the clock man and mentioned the name of Jesus, the sick man turned his face to the wall. Mr. Allison explained to him fully the way of salvation, but he seemed to pay no attention. Day after day, that missionary went to that tiny room full of germs, hot as an oven, trying to tell the dying man the wonderful story of Jesus Christ.

I sent word to Dr. Mary Stone, a very dear Chinese physician friend of mine, who immediately asked her co-worker to take the money she had set aside to buy watermelons and other fruit for herself, and share it with him. Other Christians also wanted to help this dying man. A great deal of prayer went up on his behalf.

The faithful Mr. Allison sat by his bed day after day, telling him about Jesus. Suddenly one day the man turned to him and said, "Is it possible for me to enter that beautiful heaven that you describe?"

"Yes! The Bible says in John 3:16 that whosoever believes may be saved," Mr. Allison said.

"I have been listening with my back to you day after day, ignoring you," the sick man said, "but you never gave up on me. Jesus took pity upon me and opened my heart. I am accepting Him now. I don't want to wear that blue funeral gown hanging on the door. I want to enter heaven in a white gown, because I am cleansed by the blood of Christ now."

Praise the Lord, even though Charles Leaman was in heaven by then, his clock still spoke and brought people to the Lord.

EIGHT

God Is Able

The day after Miss Leaman entered prison, word came that three old people had already died—there was no mention of names. Rumors were everywhere. I moved to an attic, dependent on others to care for me in my continuing illness until Miss Leaman would return.

Prisoners depended largely on what could be sent to them by those outside. I didn't have anything to send her except two tins of jam which she had seldom touched anyway. What was I to do? If she didn't receive anything when other prisoners received their packages, what would she think? A Swedish missionary advised, "You have to send it to the Red Cross through someone like me who is neutral. They forward it to the prisoners." I had a little empty box in which I put the jam and packed some leftover charcoal around it, marking it for "Prisoner Mary Leaman." That was the first package I had ever sent anyone!

Chinese money devaluated fast. Even an empty tin cost six hundred dollars. Meanwhile, the China Inland Mission headquarters had to be closed, and many items were being auctioned. A friend bought me twelve dozen beautiful quart jars and a German food grinder. These were a great help. Every month it was my greatest joy to get a package ready for Miss Leaman. I sold everything I could, and the Lord wonderfully provided.

Friends were able to purchase big, fat Peking dates for me. I steamed them, cooled them, and packed them tight in the jars. Then I got peanuts, fried them, shelled them, and got a friend to help me grind them on my new grinder into peanut butter. Miss Leaman didn't care for sweet things, so I put a little salt in it. I prepared food that would not require cooking or even hot water. There was a fifty-pound limit.

Many of my friends could not understand why I sent such a quantity each month when Miss Leaman could not eat much. But I knew that she wanted to help other prisoners who might not get anything. After the prisoners were released, many wrote of how much they appreciated the things I had sent to Miss Leaman. Several said that their husbands were diabetic and could eat no regular Japanese prepared food. They depended on what I sent her. She always shared her best foods with the sick.

Daily the prisoners had to pick out the rice from floor sweepings that were full of dirt and mold. They then put potato peelings and carrot skins with the moldy rice and cooked it in a big pot. They had to line up and hold out their buckets to receive the food.

Every morning at roll call, the prisoners had to stand straight, arms down. If anyone moved a finger or a foot, they were beaten. It was very cruel because those old and sick folks could not stand straight. It was especially hard for Miss Leaman, then sixty, with her spinal condition and crippled body. But she trained herself and prayed that she could stand motionless during the roll call. Later I learned that every prisoner except Miss Leaman was beaten.

Two difficult years somehow passed. One quiet afternoon a pastor's wife told me, "I have heard Miss Leaman's voice!"

"What do you mean?" I cried.

"The Japanese have surrendered, and the prisoners are free! She called me to notify you that she is free."

I was so stunned I forgot where I was and who I was. I had waited and waited for her for so long that this surprise was too much of a shock to my system. It took me a long time to recover. All the kind Chinese friends who had come to see her off to prison now were able to go into the prison to visit her. From morning until night a stream of sympathetic friends came to tell me that Miss Leaman was free and to report to me whatever news they could about her. That taxed my strength to the uttermost as I lay sick in bed. Every day I was so exhausted, yet I had such a longing that she would now be back any moment.

But day after day, she still did not come back. Why? I waited and waited. Friends came and went, and I begged them to tell me why she did not come home yet. They didn't know. "Are there other prisoners still there?" I asked anxiously.

"No, just one or two are left. All the others are free and gone."

"Well, why can't she come home?" No one could tell me.

After more than a month of anxiety, I was frantic. Her little room had been ready for so long. At eleven o'clock one night a friend brought a big, beautiful basket of fresh flowers and said, "Congratulations, Miss Tsai. Miss Leaman will return!" That false hope aggravated my delicate condition so that my exhaustion began to turn into a feeling of greater illness.

Before dawn I started to have a chill and shook for about an hour and a half. A former Buddhist nun, who had been converted by my bedside, heard my trouble, rushed to me, and held me in her arms. "Don't be afraid, Miss Tsai, the

Lord is with you!" she said. I still shook. Then I dropped into unconsciousness.

Seeing my critical condition, a friend rushed to the prison to tell Miss Leaman my situation. The prison was in the suburbs, a long way from the city of Shanghai. Another friend happened to be driving back to the city, so Miss Leaman, picking up only her Bible, left the prison with him. She lay in the back of his car and asked that he drive her to the American consulate.

Now the mystery was being solved. The American prisoners, by regulations, were all examined by American doctors before being allowed to leave the prison. When Miss Leaman was examined, her back was so bad that the doctor ordered her to be flown at once to America.

At the consulate she asked permission to have her return to America waived to allow her to stay with me for a while. "My adopted daughter is very sick," she said.

"No!" declared the consul. "You are ordered to fly back to America immediately. There are no exceptions. It is for your own good, because you need medical care and recovery. I will not allow you to stay here!"

She said she would not leave me because she was the only relative I had. He did not relent. In her extreme weakness, she sat on the hard bench at the consulate all day and waited and waited. Finally the time came for the consul to leave. The door had to be closed. She still stubbornly sat there. What a pitiful sight she must have been—so weak, thin, sick, and tired. What a love from the Lord she must have had in her heart for me! The consul was finally so frustrated with her that he disgustedly gave her permission to stay for only three months longer.

She thanked him, got up, and walked a mile to where I was living, an unbelievable feat in her condition! When she

came to my bedside at last after two years, I was so delirious
with fever that I called her "Big Brother." Somehow I had
enough presence of mind to hand her a bag with all the
records of how much money I borrowed from friends,
amounting to about $3,000 U.S. currency. When the rumor
spread that I was dying, friends came by to be sure Miss
Leaman knew how much money I had borrowed from
them.

One day a missionary who didn't identify himself came to
see me. I was unconscious, so he gave Miss Leaman a package. She asked him if he wanted a receipt, but he refused.
"No, no, I know she is a Christian," he said. The package
contained exactly $3,100 U.S. currency! How marvelously
God provided! With $400 she bought a refrigerator, which
really saved our lives. After being in prison, Miss Leaman
was very hungry but couldn't eat much at a time. That
refrigerator was a great help to us both.

Now she had money to consult many doctors about me.
No one could diagnose my illness. My fever went up to 106
degrees Fahrenheit. One doctor told Miss Leaman, "Please
do not trouble to call me again. Miss Tsai is beyond help.
Even if you called all the doctors in Shanghai, they could not
save her! There is only one last doctor for you to try, a
brilliant young man who, when he arrived in Shanghai, got
polio. He has had both legs amputated. Since he cannot
practice, he has devoted his time to laboratory work, spe-
cializing in malaria research."

Miss Leaman was desperate, since I was again at the point
of death. She called this young doctor, and he came with his
father and two nurses. "I want to give Miss Tsai a sternal
puncture," he told her. "It might be about five inches long,
about as thick as a baby's finger." He gave me an injection
near my collar bone to deaden the pain. The doctor held my

arm, the nurses tried to count my pulse, and he drilled an instrument into my bone. When he pulled it out, the blood was as black as ink. The nurses took turns stopping up the wound from which the blood oozed. It took another half hour to stop it.

The doctor told Miss Leaman, "There is no hope at all; the blood is black. I don't even need to go to the lab. It is full of malaria germs." He turned to me and said, "I'm sorry, Miss Tsai, you will die in this room."

I could only whisper, "God is able."

He said, "Miss Leaman, don't bother any more doctors. Giving her any more medicine would be just like pouring a cup of water on a burning house. It is absolutely no use." Later he sent the lab report anyway. There are thirty-six kinds of malaria germs. I had three of the most severe kinds, male and female, with generations already multiplying. The red corpuscles were being destroyed so the blood had become black.

The war had just ended. Many GIs had contracted malaria; row on row of them were lying helpless in hospitals without relief. It was then that some doctors in America finally discovered an effective medicine. They didn't dare publish its name, but only referred to it by a number. A doctor telephoned Miss Leaman, informing her that if she could find out where to get that medicine, it might be tried as a last resort. He gave her its number, but no name, for fear the Japanese would get it.

Miss Leaman suddenly remembered that when she was entering prison, a Chinese gentleman had given her his name, address, and telephone number. He had asked her to write him if she got to America, because he wanted to go, too. Not daring to keep all the address on one piece of paper, she tore it up and hid the pieces among the pages of her Bible. The Lord helped her to retrieve the pieces and put them together. When she tried phoning him, sure enough, he answered the phone himself! She asked if he knew anywhere she could find the medicine.

"It just so happens that a friend of mine returned from America only yesterday," he said. "America won't allow anyone to bring cash to China, but you may bring things like medicine, watches, et cetera. My friend brought back all kinds of medicine and things for resale. I'll go to see him. If he has brought something like that, I'll phone you."

He phoned later, saying, "Yes, my friend got one bottle of this medicine, numbered such and such. It is marked one thousand pills. The prescription says that it takes only ten pills for a cure, but my friend insists that he has to sell the whole bottle at once. The price is $350 U.S. currency. Take it or leave it!"

Miss Leaman prayed, "Dear Lord, please provide." She bought the whole bottle and immediately called the doctor. He took ten pills and ground them into powder to force down my throat. I had not been able to swallow, but somehow I managed to get this down. In a day or so, the fever went down to 104 degrees. The doctor came back to consult Miss Leaman. "Ten pills was supposed to be a cure; but since her case is so critical, shall we force another ten pills?" he asked. They agreed, and on the fifth day they tried to get me to open my mouth to take it again. By this time I had recovered a little of my understanding, but I still could not swallow at will. They had to force it down again.

After a few days the fever went down to 102 degrees. By then I was conscious and finally knew what was going on. You can imagine how I looked by that time. My face was broken out all over and my body was emaciated and in a terrible condition. I could not move a finger for six months.

The doctor said he had never seen a case as severe as mine, so he decided, "Give her three pills a day and see what happens." This continued until all one thousand pills went down! This was an unbelievable dose for any human body to absorb, let alone my tiny, frail one! Even then my fever still lingered between 100 and 101 degrees.

A lady Dr. Woo, who lived near us, was a medical doctor, and her husband was a surgeon. She kindly came twice a day to give me intravenous feedings because I could not eat. Though she had been an atheist, at Christmastime she announced to her family that she had become a Christian from watching how God had brought me back from the grave. Once she asked me, "Did you know that your family had been summoned to your deathbed and cried over you?" I said I had no such recollection. She told me that the only sign of life was that my shoulder moved a little. "In such a condition you were, and you are still here! I told my atheist family that my son and I had decided to follow the living God."

Then she asked me a favor. "Instead of my coming to give you an injection, will you let my husband come? Let him also see what a living God there is. I want him to believe in the Lord Jesus, too."

"No," I begged, "in my weakened condition I would rather have you." She continued to ask me, and the inner voice of the Spirit impressed me that I should let him come in spite of my own inconvenience. The tenderhearted Dr. Woo, her husband although an unbeliever, was a wonderful man. Every day he continued to give me injections. When my head was clearer, I shared with him about the Lord.

One day he suggested a new method of medication that might lead to a cure. He asked me if I would be willing to try it. I said that I would do anything that might help me. So every day he gave me three kinds of antimalaria medicine in three injections. Then he changed off and gave me injections for leprosy, syphillis, and snake poison.

"Doctor, I don't have all that trouble!" I complained.

He explained that he had to use poison to counteract poison, and that I had a body full of poison. The Lord helped me to again survive all those injections in my frail body. Finally I grew so sick that I couldn't eat. Struggling day after day, I became as weak as a rag. Oh, how I longed to get well! Then I started to get reactions and vomited morning to evening as if my insides had become a fountain. Kind Dr. Woo sat beside me, holding a cracker. "Just take a half piece," he urged, "even though you may vomit, some will stay down." I couldn't even talk any longer, the vomiting continued so hard.

Outside the rain was pouring. "Well, Miss Tsai," he said, "on the way to your house I learned a lesson. I saw a building that had been halfway erected, but the rain had interrupted construction. The builders had to wait until the rain stopped. I suppose we have to follow the example of that building and stop injections until you get a little better. Then we'll start again." What a relief! Little by little, oh, so slowly, I began to improve, and by and by I could eat a bit. Eventually the fever disappeared and my skin turned a sickly yellow. It was many, many months before I was once more just out of danger—temporarily!

For sixteen years my condition had scarcely changed, and there was little hope for me to be much better. Then the Lord wonderfully caused a change to take place. Miss Leaman wrote about it to her family in America in August of 1947:

I can hardly believe it is true, but day by day we watch Christiana coming back to life and strength! We bow our heads in wonder and thanksgiving for all that God has done. As the terrible pain and indescribable suffering have lessened and flesh has come on her bones once again, and her movements become free, we realize that the Lord has wonderfully preserved her in body, mind and spirit through so many years. These terrible malaria germs in her bones which bound her in weakness are diminishing and, as they decrease, she gains. The Lord in His great loving kindness and mercy seems to be restoring to her "the years that the locust hath eaten," Joel 2:25.

As she lies there she does not look older than she did before this illness came upon her! Let us pray and ask many to pray that this restored life may be used just as the Lord sees best. It is a great trust not only for her but also for us who have prayed with her through these long years of pain. May each day and each moment be used in the Lord's service just exactly as He desires.

NINE

Flight

The war closed in around us in Shanghai, and conditions grew worse. We were forced to consider fleeing China for the United States. Fear gripped the hearts of Chinese and foreigners alike. The Japanese had been a terrible threat from outside of China, but now there was an even more dangerous threat from within. It was the Communist party, which had set itself in opposition to the republican government of President Chiang Kai-shek.

Most of our friends had fled while they could. Miss Leaman had repeatedly booked passage for America, but each time we had to cancel. In my weak and painful condition, I told her I didn't think it was possible for me to go anywhere. "But you go," I urged her. "Remember how the Japanese put you in the concentration camp. It may happen again with the changing government—or worse. I am Chinese. Somehow I will be all right."

"No!" she said firmly. "I will die here with you if necessary!"

One day there was a knock on my door. An aggressive and good-looking young Chinese man asked to see me. He pushed his way in. "I am on a special errand. We want you to join our party," he demanded.

"Can't you see that I'm old and sick?" I replied. "What use would I be to any political party?"

64

He pulled out books and magazines and newspapers. "Is that your name?" He pushed them at me, showing me all the pamphlets and articles I had written after high school. "We want you to stay in China and write for our political party. You must join the party. I will come to see you again!"

He left, but the next day a different man came, repeating the same demand. The third day, still another man came. I notified my family and friends, and they answered as if with one voice, "Go! Get out of China! We would rather see you die on the ocean than to see you in their hands!"

I thought this over and prayed fervently for the Lord's wisdom. I was only one person. I should not stay and endanger my friends and my family. I asked Miss Leaman whether we should try to go to the American consulate to get our passports before we tried again to book passage on the boat. A friend of mine, who had a limousine, heard that I wanted to go to the consulate. We needed to ask the consul if we could take a servant along to America. If not, there would be no way I could survive there because of all the care that I required. The trip across town was complicated and exhausting.

At sixty-nine years of age, Miss Leaman was unusually energetic as she climbed the consulate steps. I thought to myself, *She is stronger than I; she will have many more years than I to serve the Lord. It will be all right if I am left behind and she continues to serve the Lord in America.* The consul flatly refused to let her take a servant along. She reported this to me, said that we should go home, and added, "You said that you would not consider leaving if you could not take a servant along. So we can't go."

"Wait," I said. "since we are here, it won't hurt if I go with you to see the consul." Miss Leaman, my servant, and another friend held me up so I could get on the elevator.

The lady at the desk said, "You are very wise to go while you still can. But you must see the doctor first. He is the one to say whether you can go or not."

I had seen so many, many doctors. But this was the first one with such a long American face, chewing gum all the time. In his waiting room were about thirty people. Each one was loudly arguing with him about why he would not allow him to go. He paid no attention, but just kept chewing his gum. When my turn came, he told me to lie on a high, hard table. There was such a strong light above me that I could hardly stand it.

"What happened to your hair?" he barked. I wanted to tell everything truthfully. I told him that while ill with malaria and high fever I lost all my hair. "Why is your skin so yellow?" I told him it was from the antimalarial medicine I took during my long illness. He examined me carefully. "The first finger on your left hand and the thumb on your right hand both have fungus. You must go to a surgeon and have the nails taken away from the roots, then come back to see me."

Miss Leaman was shocked and wanted to argue with the doctor. But I waved at her and said in Chinese that we should not say anything. We went to see our good friend Dr. Woo, the atheist surgeon. He was very kind and told me that according to regulations I should go to the hospital, but he would try to operate on my fingers in my own room. Three friends came to see me in tears and went with Miss Leaman into another room to pray while I had my operation. I can't describe such intense pain! To have one's fingernails cut off was torture.

We returned and I passed the consul's exam and he approved my visa. How many papers we had to sign! When we came home it was dark and we were exhausted. Evidently the bandages on my fingers had worked loose, and by bedtime sharp pains started in both of my hands. My servant, Little King, was with me all night long. I couldn't sleep a minute because of the pain. Miss Leaman and I both had phones in our rooms, but I did not want to disturb her. Just before daybreak she came to check on me, and I had to confess that I had not slept all night. She looked at my hands and turned pale. "Hurry! Send for the doctor!" she said.

The infection had gone right up into my arm about five inches, and it was swollen, white and tight. The doctor could hardly talk when he saw it. His face was like a sheet. "Miss Tsai, I'm very sorry," he said. "You must go to the hospital quickly and have part of your arm amputated!"

Miss Leaman and I could neither talk nor cry. Others scolded the doctor for being so bold as to think he could perform such a delicate and dangerous operation as removing my fingernails outside the hospital.

"Miss Tsai, there is only one other chance," Dr. Woo said. "If you are willing to cooperate, I can try to operate again. If the infection could be released downward instead of going up, there is a chance."

I agreed weakly, nauseated from the infection, and my head swimming with fever. The second operation was more terrible than the first! Again Miss Leaman went to her room in tears, pleading for the Lord's help. The pain was unbearable! The doctor made incisions in my flesh and immersed my fingers in water with strong medicine. "If the infection does not come down, we must rush you to the hospital," he warned.

Pooh, my faithful servant who was like a sister, held my hands in the basin all day and night. Every three hours for three days and three nights the doctor gave me penicillin injections. The Lord once more worked a miracle, and eventually we began to see the infection receding. Dear Pooh, never complaining or thinking of her own exhaustion, always saw to it that my hands never got out of the medicine solution. It took many weeks for my hands to recover, during which the rumors of war increased.

Finally our passports were ready. So much time had elapsed that the next boat to leave would be the last. Miss Leaman called the manager of the steamship lines. "Miss Leaman, there are three hundred on the waiting list," he said. "There is no chance!" She asked him to try his best and said she would pray.

Not too much later, the phone rang. "Miss Leaman, two passengers could not go because of illness," the manager reported. "I feel I should let you two sick people have the first chance, and I'm going to bypass the waiting list. There may be six people in your cabin, however."

"I will pray, as you try your best," Miss Leaman encouraged him. "Because we are sick, we don't want to bother others. If you could get a cabin for two, we would be very grateful."

"Impossible. Impossible," muttered the manager.

The Lord worked another miracle—we had a cabin to ourselves!

Many of our Christian Chinese friends could not leave, and they were eventually put in prison. One by one they went to be with the Lord after enduring very bravely and standing for the Lord through unimaginable trials. Many of those very friends had escorted us to the boat.

It was not easy parting from those whom we knew we would never see again on this earth. Pooh had come to me when she was only nineteen. She had served me for an additional eighteen years. As far as I remember, she never

It was our last farewell to our beloved China.

said a discourteous word to me. As we were parting, she said, "Miss Tsai, may I arrange your pillows?" choking back her sobs.

I looked at her through my own tears and whispered, "Pooh, who will arrange pillows for me after you go?" Her hot tears, big as peas, dropped on me. She had been like a sister to me. She may still be living somewhere. I often wonder—did she escape the terrors of the war and the changes that followed? Three doctors carried me to the boat.

Dr. Woo also had tears in his eyes as he held my hand. When he saw me off at the boat, he whispered, "I really hate to see you go." With so many friends around, and so much commotion, did I have time to speak a last word about the Lord to him? Yes, cost what it may, I would!

"Here is a Bible for you," I said. "I hope you will read it and that Jesus will speak to you. If you believe in Jesus, someday we will meet again in heaven." Was it any use to say once more what I had told him over and over and he had not heeded? I sent up one more earnest prayer to the Lord on his behalf and then said good-bye.

Miss Leaman and I took a last tearful farewell look at our beloved China as we were half pushed, half dragged, up the gangplank. Most presumed we would quietly fade away, and frankly I'm not sure we hoped for anything more, either. It was January 19, 1949, and we were two old, invalid women. I was fifty-nine and Miss Leaman sixty-nine.

TEN

Paradise

Several weeks later, after a stop in Honolulu and deboarding in San Francisco exhausted and ill, Miss Leaman and I traveled cross-country by train. We arrived in the predawn light of a winter's morning, and the porter swooped us off and deposited us with our baggage on the long, cold platform in Pennsylvania. Snow swirled around us, and the train pulled away, leaving us shivering and deserted. An unbelievably long flight of stairs led up to the station, and neither of us could imagine climbing them. There was nothing to do but wait and pray to be rescued.

I thought, what a difference from my first visit to America in the 1920s when Miss Leaman invited me to accompany her on one of her infrequent furloughs. Invitations came from the Presbyterian Board, asking me to make an extensive speaking tour throughout the United States. I was booked in prominent churches, Bible colleges, before the General Assembly of the Presbyterian Church, at Moody Bible Institute, to address prisoners at Sing Sing, and for an audience with President Harding, who invited me on a tour of the White House. For three years I rode on the crest of the wave of popularity and saw, with great admiration, the wide scope of Christian work everywhere in America. We stayed in mansions of wealthy Christians and in humble homes of ordinary folk. Everywhere we traveled, crowds were on hand to greet us and arrange for our comfort. The days we spent with the family at the Leaman home in Paradise were precious ones.

During that furlough there were two Mary Leamans at the old homestead, the other being a cousin. The name "China Mary" was used to distinguish the missionary Mary, the one born in China. It was particularly appropriate, because she was indeed more Chinese than American from the inside out.

Now here we were, more than two decades later, deposited like abandoned freight along the railroad tracks. After a long while, two men appeared with two wheelchairs. Thinking they were for each of us, we gladly staggered toward them. But they put me in one and our baggage in the other, evidently sizing up the situation and assuming that at least the American lady seemed to be able to walk. China Mary tottered weakly beside me, holding me up and steadying herself. I was very dizzy as usual and could easily have tumbled out of the chair. The men pushed us and our baggage in and out of two elevators, finally reaching the baggage room. Then they disappeared. I was ready to collapse. A good friend had arranged to pick us up in her car at seven o'clock. "We will be dead by that time," I whispered. "We must get a taxi at once."

After the ten-mile ride to the village of Leaman Place in Paradise, Pennsylvania, we saw the great old house lighted up from end to end to welcome us. The driveway was heaped with snow. China Mary's sister Lucy and their cousin Mary were waiting at the door. Lucy hugged and kissed us ecstatically. Cousin Mary laughed excitedly, "Welcome to Paradise!"

We had a glimpse of the front parlor full of antique furniture accumulated by the Leamans. The spacious old-fashioned kitchen with its wood-burning stove was at the back, but I was too tired to stay up. With help, I sank into the high-backed antique bed and asked for the shades to be pulled. I felt literally and figuratively in Paradise! Our days of refugeeing were over, our hardships at an end. We could rest at last. But a disturbing thought suddenly crossed my mind. Perhaps our lives of usefulness to the Lord were really at an end. What could we do for Him in this remote corner of the world?

The big, brown more than two-hundred-year-old house at Paradise was weathered but still sturdy. It nestled in a rich, rolling "garden spot" of America, Lancaster County, Pennsylvania. Christian Leaman had purchased it and an adjacent tract of land from General William Reynolds of Revolutionary War fame. He persuaded relatives and friends to build there also, and the government was so pleased that it named the village Leaman Place.

That put us on the map. This house had once been an inn where horseback riders on their way from Philadelphia to Lancaster stopped to switch horses. Lincoln Highway, Route 30, now runs past our door. It cut back our land, shaving off the front yard right up to the front porch. Oh, how I had loved the beautiful apple trees that always seemed to wave us a welcome when we got off the trolley in front of the Leaman house on our first trip to America! Now we were exposed day and night to a bombardment of trailers, ponderous trucks, and zooming motor cars which stormed up one hill and down the other in a thundering, never-ending stream.

Next door was a red brick country store, behind us a lumber yard and feed mill. A hundred yards behind our house was a freight station on the Pennsylvania Railroad, with long lines of freight cars rattling by at frequent intervals. Now speeding passenger trains zip along the gleaming

tracks of the Pennsylvania main line, no longer stopping at
the small Leaman Place station as they did a generation
ago.

All around us was the lush, rolling countryside studded
with clusters of gleaming white farm buildings, houses with
large barns and silos. All this set in emerald green fields of
waving corn, rippling wheat, and broad-leafed tobacco. Sky
and earth met along the wooded ridges that shut in our
world.

This was the country of the pink-cheeked, white-capped
Mennonite women. Here also lived the somber, bearded,
black-garbed Amish men and the bonneted, long-skirted
women. Children still dressed as miniature adults, complete
with black-brimmed hats and bonnets. Even today they are
frequently seen and heard clopping along in horse-drawn
carriages past our door, even on the traffic-laden Highway
30. Both religious groups are quiet, peace-loving, and con-
servative folk whose farms are their showcases. They still
cling to the honest pioneer tradition of plain living and good,
hard work. We get plenty of fresh fruit from their orchards,
vegetables from their gardens, and creamy milk from their
Holstein and Guernsey herds. Baked goods are brought to
our door, and other homegrown produce abounds in the
country store. We seemed to be in a Garden of Eden, and
the pain and war of China were far away.

But our hearts were still in China with those we loved and
with whom we shared Christ. My thoughts turned often to
those I'd left behind, my relatives and friends, as little iron
filings follow the magnet.

Not very long after we arrived, an airmail letter came from
Dr. Woo in China. I opened the letter anxiously. There was a
drawing of a birthday cake with candles and figure with a
Bible kneeling beside the cake. What could that mean?

Dear Miss Tsai: After we said good-bye, I went home. As you advised me, I asked the Holy Spirit to be my Teacher and immediately opened the Bible. I read and read and read; I even forgot to go to bed. Never a day passed that I didn't read it. The Lord must have heard the prayers of you and Miss Leaman. Thank you for your patience. The Bible taught me that I am a sinner. I read that there is only one way to go to Heaven and that is by believing in Jesus. That picture I drew is of me, kneeling by the Bible. I have accepted Jesus Christ as my Savior. I just wanted to let you know: that is your birthday gift! I know that probably I will never be able to come to America to see you, and you will not be able to return to China. But, as you said when we parted, one day we will meet in Heaven!

Oh, may the Lord help me, in season and out of season, when I feel like it or not, whether it is convenient or not, to tell people about Jesus. I must sow the seed—then the Lord sees to the harvest!

A year later, yet another letter arrived for me indirectly from one of my brothers left behind the bamboo curtain. He had been one who opposed my faith fiercely. He had torn up my Bible and hymnbook after my conversion and had persecuted me bitterly when I left Buddhism. He had resisted Christ for a long time. Who could have been more hardened than he?

But as he watched how the Lord tenderly led me through the severe suffering of prolonged illness in 1947, and how I faced it without complaining, the Holy Spirit began to touch his heart. The letter recounted how he had asked members of our family to gather around him. He announced, "From watching our sister's long suffering and seeing how she was given indescribable strength to bear it all, I know there must be a God! Therefore, I ask Him to forgive my sins. I decide now to follow Him and accept Him as my everlasting Saviour!"

Praise Almighty God! Churches in China may be forced to close, but the Head of the church, Jesus Christ, can never be closed out of the hearts of His true believers. Missionaries may have been driven from the visible China, but the Holy Spirit can never be driven out of His own children.

ELEVEN

The Lily

China Mary and I felt like fish out of water. We were in our pleasant American home with its many conveniences, but we were used to China ways. Housekeeping here with the help of experienced, capable women, who had good minds of their own, was a contrast to China where ignorant country folk were content to be our hands and feet.

Neither of us knew much about cooking nor had the strength to do heavy chores. Missionaries in China, as in other lands, did not usually do many of their own household tasks. They were in the country by the call of the Lord to give priority to their ministry among the people. It would not have been good stewardship of their time and efforts to spend large segments of each day in taking care of their homes while servant help was so willing, available, and inexpensive.

China Mary, although American, was indeed more Chinese in outlook and approach. She loved the Chinese people dearly. Like the Mary of Bethany in the Bible, she was deeply spiritual, devoting her life to prayer, personal counseling, and literary pursuits.

In China we always ate Chinese food, which I had our servants prepare. China Mary hardly cared what food was set before her and often forgot to eat if more important matters demanded her attention. It did not matter to her

how food tasted, as long as it was nourishing. Now, as the
eldest and least feeble of the four of us, she became head of
our household and had to learn the role of Martha in the
Bible. She had to be busy "about many things" (Luke
10:41). Yet her mind was always on the less common. Her
hardest task was to remember that there was food cooking
on the stove. How often it burned! She had to teach herself
to cook, and her inclination toward things Chinese was revealed in the tasty dishes she prepared, even ordering in-
gredients from New York or Hong Kong.

China Mary often reminded Cousin Mary, Lucy, and me
of Genesis 45:24, when the brothers of Joseph went to
Egypt to buy food. Joseph sent the brothers back to their
fathers, cautioning them, "See that ye fall not out by the
way." The Chinese translation indicates that this means not
to argue. We asked the Lord to help the four of us understand each other and not quarrel on our journey. So our
code was simple: never criticize one another, never question
motives, and never turn away an opportunity to witness for
the Lord. God never failed to do His part by blessing His
work through us.

Forced to put behind me all the comforts of my early
wealth and luxury, I have learned to simplify my way of life. I
have furnished my room with only bare essentials: a bed,
small tables, night stand, sofa and chairs for guests, a book-
case, and lamps covered by dark cloth. There is one window
with dark shades drawn. This dark chamber is my office,
dining room, reception room, and sleeping quarters. It also
becomes my meeting hall and sanctuary. My bed is the
platform from which I speak when groups come to see me.

I have to set two stages every day: so in the morning I get
my room ready for the public eye by putting away all night
things, changing clothes, and washing up. Unexpected

guests often pop in very early. At night I have to turn my chamber again into a hospital room with everything handy for me during the night when I am alone. Often in the morning, after a sleepless night and the continued pain of my illness, I have felt so weak that my tears have washed my face as I have arranged my stage for the day. Yet I did not dare to let China Mary know, lest she be anxious about me. Often a quiet voice seemed to whisper to me, "Just count your many blessings instead!"

When guests come, they are invited to sit on little wooden chairs, which we brought back from the kindergarten that Lucy taught in China. Everything has its appointed place, and I usually know where to find it. People even come to me to borrow what they need and are amazed when I generally can produce it. I still sit up in bed every morning, "waiting for biscuits" as I did when I was a child. China Mary always brought them to me with the morning mail. Before we opened our letters, we asked our heavenly Father to bless every sender and make us a blessing in our contacts with them.

Letters and guests became our life. The buzz of voices and the hum of activity were a welcomed break from the deadly monotony of a shut-in's life. They were pleasant sounds that tended to drown out the nuisance kind. We welcomed each guest with open arms. China Mary and I prayed each morning, "Lord, bring only those to us whom You desire, and keep away all who would only tax our strength and take our time away from Your ministry to the lives of those who need You."

When guests arrived, we enthusiastically received them, standing on God's promise that they were the exact ones He had sent.

Interruptions made up the business of our lives. The

neighbor who dropped in at mealtime and the stranger driving by who wanted to meet us, might both have parked their cars under the old apple tree before ringing our bell. Hundreds of guests have opened doors and windows to us on an ever widening world. Invalids like us, full of aches and pains, could have been overcome by self-pity unless we had concentrated on helping others. We soon realized that we were faced with either giving way to our symptoms and shutting out the world, or of rising above them and welcoming the interruptions, even capitalizing on them.

Though having set our feet in the latter direction, times would come when I would doubt that I could serve the Lord in my solitary room so far away from the traffic of life. I was hidden away in a dark, unknown corner. Then the Lord, to encourage me, brought to my mind an early experience that happened soon after my conversion.

By my doctor's orders, I was to take walks every day on the hilltops of Kuling, in Kiukiang, China, one of China's most beautiful summer resorts.

Early every morning I said good-bye to my spiritual mother, China Mary, and started my walk with my young maid. I wore straw sandals and carried a staff. My maid brought a little package of food, a small teakettle, and a box of matches. When we came to a stream where the clear water rippled quietly down from its fountain in the hills, we made a little fireplace with stones, gathered some twigs and branches, lighted the fire, and cooked our breakfast.

How the morning star shone brightly and beautifully! The rustling pines and topmost branches of stately trees joyously bowed to each other above the sparkling streams to welcome the rising of the gorgeous, glorious sun. "O my Creator, Maker of heaven and earth, I adore Thee, I worship

In the midst of that dirty, solitary dump stood an exquisite lily.

Thee!" was the prayer of my young heart, newly awakened
to Christ's love.

One morning my maid lingered to examine some of the
odd stones. I went on, wading through a cool stream and
climbing some rocks to a narrow path. The sound of a
waterfall spoke to my heart that I was not alone—I felt aware
of the companionship of my Lord. He was indeed al-
together lovely! I walked along, lifting my face to the blue
skies, singing, "He leadeth me." Suddenly an indescribable
sweet fragrance made me turn to discover its source. I
searched and found only an ugly rubbish pile with broken
pieces of stone discarded by stone workers in that hidden,
unkept, and unfrequented spot. To my surprise, in the midst
of that dirty, solitary dump stood an exquisite lily, incompa-
rable in its stately beauty. It shared its fragrance freely for the
joy of a chance passerby like myself.

May the God of all circumstances help me to diffuse His
fragrance right here where I am! "Now thanks be to God,
which always causeth us to triumph in Christ, and maketh
manifest the savour of his knowledge by us in every place"
(2 Corinthians 2:14). Through heavy burdens, prolonged
pain and sickness, people's misunderstandings, failing
health and strength, uncertainty about the future and financial straits, may my Lord's own sweet fragrance flow in and
out of this little darkened corner.

TWELVE

Queen of the Dark Chamber

China Mary and I were just two trickles that leaked out from China and dribbled down into a hollow in Pennsylvania. But we were a strange puddle that refused to dry up. Something had to happen here. The setting was both impossible and ideal. There was the big, brown house, secure but restricting. And there were four invalids—companionable but helpless.

We sensed a call to draw all Chinese exiles together. Old friends from China (exiles like us) passing along the road, stopped often to chat with us. We had a common faith in divine providence that makes all believers in Jesus Christ children of God and brothers and sisters in Him, regardless of race, tongue, or profession.

A common love of the Chinese way of life, with its excellent traditions of courtesy and hospitality, woke memories of good things and good times shared in the past. They were doubly precious because they were behind us and far from us. We had a common loyalty to a world we appreciated and loved, now at least temporarily lost; a mutual sorrow for the tragic plight of the Christian friends we had left behind in China; a deep concern for the dark, agonizing ordeal of China's millions. This opened up the fountains of love in our hearts. We never stopped wondering what happened to the friendly, smiling multitudes we loved. What madness of change had come over changeless China?

China was in our blood, embedded in our bones, crystalized in our thoughts, and echoing from our lips. How could we forget the latticed windows, the vermilion walls, the turned-up temple roofs, the jade green rice fields, the blue hills, the winding canals crossed by artistic arched bridges, the patched sails of the gliding junks? How could we blot out the memory of the jolly rickshaw boy with his eagerness for passengers, the song of the toiling coolie with his backbreaking load, the elegant, witty scholar with his nimble brush, the slender woman with her sleek black hair and her chubby children staring at us with solemn eyes? Just as real to us as our new friends were memories of smiling, wrinkled, old village folk, wiley merchants, the ever present throngs, the confusion of dialects, the rags and riches that are China.

"What is happening to our own friends in China?" That was the question ever springing from our anxious hearts. But it was a question no one could answer. We dared not write to any friends and relatives over there for fear of reprisals upon them. Every little scrap of information plucked from the Hong Kong grapevine was eagerly discussed and passed on. Yet the sometimes unspoken but keenly sensed questions that finally impelled me to write my first book were, "Was it worth it to send missionaries to China? Was it all in vain: the money spent, the lives invested, the earnest prayers, and the blood shed?" I had to witness! I had to confirm, to declare, to encourage, to shout that it was! Praise God, it was worth it!

But I must confess that after we were finally somewhat settled in the old Leaman homestead, and some of our personal effects were unpacked, the reality of my isolation began to grip me. I faced an "open end" confinement in a room about twelve feet wide and fifteen feet long. I had

promised the Lord that as long as I had breath I would serve
Him, and at every opportunity I would witness to the gospel. I found myself with breath, but no opportunity to go
anywhere to witness about Him. This poem echoed my
feelings:

> "Father, where shall I work today?"
> And my love flowed warm and free.
> Then He pointed me toward a tiny spot
> And said, "Tend that for me."
> I answered quickly, "Oh, no, not that!
> Why, no one would ever see.
> No matter how well my work is done:
> Not that little place for me!"
> And the word He spoke it was not stern:
> He answered me tenderly:
> "Ah, little one, search that heart of thine
> Art thou working for them or for Me?
> Nazareth was a little place,
> And so was Galilee!"

And so was Paradise, Pennsylvania! Driving through it
either from the east or west on Highway 30, a person could
miss it and be far beyond before realizing it. Having lived in
teeming cities in China much of my life, I felt I was now in
the middle of nowhere. How could I go with the gospel
when I was a shut-in who could not even walk? I laid the
problem before the Lord. I rested contentedly, because it
was His problem and not mine.

Then He began to speak through friends who knew my
story and were repeating it over and over to others. Clearer
came the conviction of His call: "Write a book to witness of
Me and reach the world."

"Lord, how can I write? And who would read it? I am
nobody. Who knows my name? In China, years ago, I was

known. But after so many years, who knows Christiana
Tsai?"

It was as if the Lord gently rebuked me by saying, "You
are not to write a book about what *you* did but what *I* did.
My name is important, not yours!"

Two years passed before I could do anything about giving
wings to my witness. I was often ill with recurrent attacks of
malaria. My head would ache so that I felt it would burst. My
dizziness swayed the room until I was seasick with nausea. I
could neither eat nor sleep. Any slight noise would jar me
into a painful consciousness. I used to dream of my old
Chinese servant. "If only Pooh were here to rub my arms!" I
sighed. "She would keep up my courage in the face of the
endless pain and boredom of lying in bed alone." In my
better moments I tried to sing hymns and keep my mind
stayed upon the Lord.

I recognized God's hand of training and preparation upon
me. In moments when I was somewhat free from pain, I
began to jot down in a notebook an outline of my early life
and the events of the Lord's working through the years.
Many months passed and my notebook grew full. One day
about two years after we had left China, Ellen Drummond,
another missionary exile from our own area, arrived in our
hollow. We were old friends and our bonds were close in
Christ. We had lived in the same war-scarred house in
Shanghai during the two years before we came to the
United States. We had been grateful that in that jam-packed
city we had a roof over our heads and four walls around us.

Miss Drummond also was a second-generation missionary, her parents having come to Nanking, China, later than
the Leamans. She now also shared with us the dubious
distinction of ill health—one more cripple, though not a
shut-in.

When I told her my decision to write my life story, she offered to help. Ellen was retired now and so had leisure time. Above all, she knew us intimately, as well as the setting and scenes of our lives from childhood. For me, cooped up in that dark room, it seemed that my only contribution to spreading the gospel from this point on could be my personal testimony. I could recount the great things God had done for me, my family, and fellow Chinese countrymen through the Christian missionaries.

While I was unable to realize my heart's desire to travel around America as I had done in the 1920s testifying of God's grace, I could still express my gratitude to Him through the written page. The story of my life would be carried into the homes and hearts of people everywhere. Perhaps this book would encourage many faithful believers who had prayed so fervently and given so sacrificially for mission work in China in the past, and who were now asking whether all the labor there had been in vain.

The theme of my story would center around the mighty work of God wrought by His Spirit in the place of greatest darkness. I would testify that although I was privileged to come from a wealthy, aristocratic family of imperial China, a product of its ancient historic culture and pride, Buddhism did not hold the answer to my heart's need. As a young girl I had no inner peace, no enlightenment. I was almost ready to take my vows to enter the Lin-yin Convent and become a nun. My superior nun had already given me a new name. The day had been set for shaving my hair and entering the "gates of emptiness." But the God whom I did not yet know had other plans. He had prepared a new name for me, too, to be written in the Lamb's book of life. He detoured me around the rocks of Buddhism and guided me directly to the Rock of Ages.

Since coming to know Christ, my greatest joy became to win others to Him, beginning with the members of my own big family. I knew there were many in America who also had no peace, in spite of materialistic abundance; many who suffered without hope; many lonely souls who felt they were no longer wanted. I knew they could all find peace in Christ. My story would help them. So with Ellen's help, we set upon our demanding task.

It seemed impossible, but with God's ever present help and nearly round-the-clock writing, we finished the first draft in two short months. The first great step had been taken in a chain of events that was to grow in ever widening circles—spreading to more and more parts of the world even to this day. However, the manuscript was far from ready to be submitted to a publisher. We needed line-by-line correction and polish, to which the four of us shut-ins applied ourselves every day for a whole year. After a quick breakfast, we would all gather in my room and pray for God's guidance in each word, each thought, each paragraph. Then we would spend hour after hour working with care on accuracy and continuity. We wanted every event to be recorded to the glory of God and not man. Cousin Mary often remarked, "If this book is ever published, it will be a book of prayer!"

My eyes could not read continually, so the three Leamans patiently took turns reading each paragraph to me. So often I said, "Please read it again."

Finally we reached the point of needing an expert typist for the final draft. One spry, ninety-two-year-old judge's wife and resident of Lancaster had been writing down historical notes about Lancaster. She came to see us once in a while, always chauffeured by her niece. This young lady was a meticulous businesswoman, charming to look at, and dressed in the most attractive fashion. As she sat on the little kindergarten chair by my bed, I talked with her about missions. She coldly and brusquely stated, "I am not a Christian. I am not interested in missions."

At this rebuff I prayed silently, *Fisher of men, perhaps I am not the right bait for this fish,* and I did not press her further. She left me and went into the parlor to join the others.

Later China Mary hurried breathlessly into my room with the news. "That young lady has offered to type your manuscript free of charge! She says she can come every Saturday to go over it with you!"

The following Saturday and each Saturday thereafter, she arrived, beautifully dressed in a different stylish outfit each time. She carefully and expertly went over every comma, period, and quotation mark in the manuscript. Later, much to my great surprise, she said, "Your story is interesting. The people in my office gather around my table and ask me to read it aloud."

Another week a missionary, who accompanied her out of my room, heard her remark, "Anyone who did not believe in Jesus before could not help believing after reading that book."

Later she made an even more electrifying announcement. "I have already asked to be baptized," she said, quickly adding, "But I don't want to be a missionary. I don't want to leave my country."

"Dear lady, we are all missionaries," I said.

She opened her eyes wide and asked plaintively, "Do I have to be one?"

"Yes!" I said, but then inquired, "Do you love your husband?"

"Of course," she replied, puzzled.

"As long as you do, you will work in the kitchen. And you can start by being an in-kitchen missionary," I told her. "I myself cannot go traveling around the country, but I am still an in-bed missionary."

By God's grace we had now completed the manuscript, but we had not decided on a publisher. I had always admired Moody Bible Institute since I studied Moody correspondence courses years ago in China. My first choice was to send it to Moody Press. A pastor who had been a salesman for seven years in a well-known bookstore, said, "Publishing is a gamble. The life of such a book is short—six months to a year. Moody Press only publishes books by well-known people. Nobody knows you," he warned.

"People may not know me," I said, "but my God knows me. I heard that when Queen Elizabeth and Princess Margaret were children they lost their way and landed at an old folks home. 'Who are you?' an old man asked them. 'We are nobodies,' they replied, 'but our father is king!' "

China Mary and I prayed about it and mailed the manuscript to Moody Press. Two months later the acceptance came! In August 1953, *Queen of the Dark Chamber* was off the press. Seven months later it had already been reprinted three times.

THIRTEEN

Best Seller

From 1953 to 1976, *Queen of the Dark Chamber* was reprinted thirty-six times in English by Moody Press and translated into more than thirty forms of publication and two Braille editions. Many best sellers have had far greater circulation, but we had the assurance that God was sending this particular witness to every individual whose heart He had already prepared.

The Lord's gift to us was a renewed interest in life and many friends. I am busy from morning until night. Countless friends from far and near, in fact, from all over the world, have made my life richer, sweeter, and brighter. Because some message in my book stirred their hearts, they have been drawn over the highways and down into our hollow.

As book sales mounted, enthusiastic reviews appeared in magazines. The postman began stuffing our box full of "fan mail." One letter was from John F. Kullgren of Washington, D.C.:

Dear Miss Tsai:

I saw your book, *Queen of the Dark Chamber*. And as I read, it suddenly dawned upon me that here I was meeting once again that childhood "Queen" of the lighted temple: an unforgettable, charming, persuasive, no less than dramatic messenger of the Gospel, who suddenly appeared in my small-children circle, who conquered me wholly—and then, somehow, disappeared among the 450 million Chinese, not to reappear before now. Yes, I conclude from reading the book about you, that you must be that person. I thought you might like to read about our last meeting:

It must have been about 1915 or 1916, when I was a 10-year-old schoolboy at the Swedish School in Ichang, Hupeh Province. At the time, my parents, of the Swedish Missionary Society, were in Wuchang, and I was at the school in Ichang, living with Rev. Fernstrom and his wife, who were in charge of us children. One day this beautiful Chinese young lady appeared, living with us at the mission while conducting an evangelistic campaign.

You not only aroused the Chinese congregation of the various Swedish and British missions in Ichang, you roused us Swedish children as well to a new desire to confess our sins and become "living" Christians. You used to sit down by the organ in the parlor of the "Ladies House," and teach us a song which you liked. And we learned your song by routine, the way Chinese school children learned their characters by endless repetition. And I'm not sure now that I know the meaning of all the words in the song, no more than the Chinese children necessarily knew the meaning of all the characters they repeated. But your song has stuck in my memory all these years, and that should show a good teacher as well as a willing student.

These were sounding words, written and sung for a people who still largely went to their Buddhist and Taoist temples and had to be given the reassurance of Christian, heavenly, protection in order to desist from their tradition-bound ways. Not that we children went praying to these temples! The point of learning the song was that it was your song, and when you led, we followed gladly. We were all, and I for certain, caught by that evangelistic revival spirit of yours. But most of all, that refreshing memory of you has never dimmed. To the boy, you were a princess from a Chinese fairyland, brought up-to-date in a twentieth century reality. Aptly, in the book about you, you are now a queen.

Reading the book about you not only recalls that China from World War I and before World War II which we loved so much. It also provides a personal inspiration, retracing your life of devotion to your people and unswerving faith in the gospel of Christ, a faith I know will continue to sustain you in this period of trials you have sustained through these many late years of sickness. It is so sad to read this part of your book, but though our science lacks means of healing you, it is clear that your spirit and your faith are sustaining you to bear these sufferings without a waver of your enthusiasm for life and the furtherance of the fellowship of man under Christ.

Suddenly life was transformed. The prayer that China Mary and I first offered when we began serving the Lord together many years ago became an even greater heart cry now that we faced the throngs of people the Lord was bringing to us. Now we prayed, "May the Lord whom we love and serve together this day, suggest, direct, and control all that we say and do for Him and for His children."

We were no longer just overage freighters, rusting away at our anchors. We soon had to have our driveway enlarged. Many visitors were old missionary friends, delighted to find us again. They dropped in without ceremony as they were passing by. Many church delegations phoned for engagements. Sometimes Sunday school youngsters came to sing for us. Whole families stopped by to say hello and then stayed for a meal. Travelers saw the JESUS SAVES sign in both English and Chinese in our yard and wanted to talk over their problems. Groups of college students on vacation arrived. Church leaders on the way to conferences enjoyed refreshment at our home.

A little boy of ten, who came with his grandfather, a retired general of the United States Army, promised to send me a dollar a month. I called him "president of my mission board." I told my boy president, "Hereafter I cannot say that since 1919 I serve my Lord only by faith since I expect to receive one dollar a month regularly from you!"

We were honored that numerous dignitaries—political, educational, military, and religious—visited us. Indians, Japanese, Koreans, and many from the Philippines have taken the trouble to find us Visitors come in the front door and the back door. Sometimes we have one guest at a time, although frequently we have several groups in the house at once. On special occasions the hall, sitting room, and kitchen have been full, and there has barely been standing room in my bedroom, with the overflow gathering at my door.

An interested friend examined our guest books over a period of a month and figured our average to be about forty-three guests daily!

Many were earnest Christians who had much to give us in inspiration and fellowship. Some were sick, searching for health, and some were burdened, asking for prayer, while a number were just curious "to see the little Chinese girl" they had heard about. Wide-eyed children asked to see this mysterious "queen" who lived in a dark room. To tell the truth, my life, while unusual, has had more downs than ups, but to them it sounded exotic and glamorous. I was surely no longer a girl, nor a queen, just an ordinary person, and well into my sixties.

Visitors were a challenge that we could not refuse, but you can imagine that we were taxed to the utmost. Often I trembled to answer the phone. Lucy was under doctor's orders to keep quiet. Cousin Mary had been sheltered all her life. Only China Mary, a strange blend of iron determination and simple faith, never wavered. She decreed that we would receive and entertain, in the best Christian and Leaman family tradition, everyone who came. Nothing was too good for our guests.

Fortunately, we all enjoyed meeting people. So we rose little by little to meet the challenge, each entertaining in her own way. Such interesting and worthwhile guests they proved to be! They have done far more for us than we could have done for them. Each of our shut-in quartet rallied at the sound of the doorbell and found untapped resources of spiritual power and physical stamina to bear up under the strain. Many neighbors pitched in and helped to serve refreshments. Food had to be stocked so we could be ready at a moment's notice. The dining room table usually remained extended to accommodate perpetual guests. Then, after the meal, the inevitable dishes had to be washed.

China Mary was busy from morning till night. She still wore Chinese clothes, usually of navy blue, and rarely had time to take off her apron in an entire day. Always quiet, always smiling, always unhurried, she devoted herself to each individual, no matter who he was. Butcher, baker, truck driver, or repairman, was always prayed with at the door before he left. Though they were busy people, most appreciated it. With all visitors she was the perfect hostess, greeting them warmly, sitting down with them quietly, conversing about the Lord. If they arrived at mealtime, they were simply included, and when they had to go, she urged them to return soon. "Restful availability" was China Mary's motto—available to the Lord for His gentle leading through her to touch the lives of others for His glory.

One man driving by had noticed our sign. He was an alcoholic. "Your sign said that Jesus saves. Can this Jesus save me?" he asked. China Mary sat down in the parlor and talked and prayed with this absolute stranger for two hours. He came back the next day to thank her. "It worked! It worked!" he reported gratefully. "I gave my problem to Jesus!"

I am often cautioned by my doctor to keep the flow of visitors to a minimum so as not to overtax my frail body and mind. But he has begun to realize through many years of caring for me that God's Spirit in me is still vigorous, although very evidently my "outer man" is wasting away. When China Mary would come into my room to say, "Dear, there are some visitors who want to see you," no matter how weary I had been the moment before, no matter how I ached, I would come to life and begin to organize: I would comb my hair, change into my black velvet jacket, spread out my silken coverlet over my work on the bed, and ask to have chairs arranged. Then I would set out my Bible and books and other things that I might want to refer to, and genuinely welcome the visitors and treat them like long-lost friends.

I am not blind, but since bright light hurts my eyes, there is a covered light by my bed and another shaded one by the window. I cannot see people's faces very clearly as they come in, only their shadowy outlines. At most, only thirty can be seated in my room on folding chairs, but on frequent occasions forty or more are squeezed in. More than once the over one-hundred-year-old bed has cracked with the weight of extra guests sitting beside me! Many other guests stand in the dining room looking in.

But whether my guests are adults or children, men or women, important people or simple folk, we like to have them talk about themselves and tell us what is on their hearts. Interesting discussions develop, and all kinds of questions are asked—some on theology, world affairs, spiritual subjects, and even medical matters.

Even in my advanced age, I still get nervous and apprehensive when people I don't know descend upon me. In myself I know that I have nothing to give them. I often feel inadequate to share Christ with those who are well educated, knowledgeable in world affairs, and probably preachers and teachers themselves. But the Lord reminds me that it is not myself I am to present to them, but Himself. Then He takes care of the butterflies in my stomach that are flitting about because of my lifelong fear of strangers. Has not God's Word declared, "Be not afraid of their faces" (Jeremiah 1:8)?

One spring I had accepted an appointment with twenty-two medical doctors and nurses from hospitals in the Philadelphia area. One doctor had been here before. After only a short time of fellowship in the Lord, we all became warm friends as if we had known each other all our lives. They bought one hundred and twenty copies of my book to share with their friends. They were convinced that many of their patients and suffering ones, after reading my testimony of God's keeping power, would be moved by the Lord to courageously go on.

Three days later, twenty-five members and campus leaders of Inter-Varsity Christian Fellowship spent some time with me. Although none of us had ever met before, again we were wonderfully united in the Lord.

Menno Simon, one of our dear Mennonite friends and a well-known businessman, was critically ill in the hospital some distance from us in Pennsylvania. China Mary phoned him every day to pray with him. For three weeks his pain grew so severe that he could hardly stand it.

China Mary asked me, "Do you feel led to pray not only for his freedom from pain, but also for his healing?" He had been praying that the Lord would show him if there was anything in his life that had caused this suffering, that he might deal with it before the Lord, or else that his pain might be relieved.

I answered, "Yes, but he must agree in faith with us." We phoned him with our proposal and he agreed. We three formed a prayer circle. He had not slept through the night for many weeks because of the pain, always depending on tranquilizers and injections to get any rest at all. Then China Mary and I prayed for him through the night, pleading God's promises according to His Word and according to His will.

Menno phoned us the next day, relating this wonderful story:

"Last night, although still in intense pain, I suddenly fell sound asleep. But soon I woke up and lay quietly, not daring to believe that my pain was gone! The nurse came in to give me my usual injection to relieve the pain and I refused it. 'I have no more pain,' I insisted. She could hardly believe it when I got right out of bed and walked around. Later the doctor came in. 'I have bad news for you,' he said, shaking his head seriously. 'We don't know what is wrong with you, but we know that we can't give you the every-four-hour pain killer any longer because your system can't take it.' I told the astonished doctor, 'That's all right. I don't need it—I'm perfectly well!'"

We thanked the Lord together on the phone for His healing. In two days he was discharged from the hospital, and the pain has never returned. Menno Simon, a sincere, hardworking Christian before, rededicated his life and all that he had from the Lord to serve Him even more faithfully.

FOURTEEN

My Co-workers

A house is not self-cleaning. Meals don't appear out of thin air. Dishes don't jump up and wash themselves. How could all these activities go on with crowds of extra guests in a house of invalids? We can invite people to a meal, but someone has to buy the food, prepare and serve it. When people drop in at all hours of the day and night, someone must give extra time to attend to them.

It is the dear friends and co-workers among the Mennonites who have touched our lives so deeply since we settled in America, and without whom we would not have survived. When any guests have visited us, they are first met by Mennonites who help us in our home. Often they are also entertained in Mennonite homes and taken to their places of worship. Their testimonies have made a lasting impression on many of our friends, especially the Chinese students and military officers.

The Mennonite women have been "ministering angels" to us. They have expressed the serenity and peace of the Lord not only in their faces but in their hearts. They have the kind of happiness, peace, and assurance in their lives that most people desire. They are well known for their orderly and spotless houses and their neat buildings, yards, fences, and gardens. Because they are not afraid of hard work and center their interest in home tasks, they immediately came to our rescue. They helped us at every turn with cooking, cleaning, physical care, and their generous hospitality to the many visitors whom the Lord brought to us. They lived a Christlike life before our guests and ministered God's Word to them as well.

In China, a friend who knew our circumstances said firmly, even prophetically, "I am praying that God will provide you with some Mennonites in America who will work with you." That is just what happened!

Miss Susanna Eshleman, our neighbor, is a Mennonite lady and faithful follower of the Lord Jesus who recognized our need and came to help us with housekeeping. She soon learned our Chinese ways of living and became accustomed to meeting internationals and people from different walks of life. Friends often tell me how kind and thoughtful she is. Hostess, companion, prayer partner, nurse, cook, and housekeeper are only a few of her many ministries. Whenever unexpected callers drop in around mealtime, it is Susanna who has to leave her work and prepare a meal for them. Having had much experience in nursing members of her own family in the past, she helped nurse each of us invalid four with faithful dedication.

After my book was published I desperately needed someone to help me with my exploding correspondence. The Lord provided a second Mennonite friend, Mrs. Frances Stoltzfus, a farmer's wife and busy mother of three daughters. She drives the sixteen-mile round trip to our home several times a week, no matter what the weather, to do my secretarial work. Her sacrificial devotion has made possible the extensive correspondence related to the worldwide distribution of my book and its various printings and foreign editions. She sits at the foot of my bed in the semidarkness and takes dictation. She writes faster than I can dictate and then transcribes my letters in the parlor on a portable typewriter. She has attended to the packing and mailing of thousands of book orders through the years, and as a personal secretary she handles much of my business. In the early days of our working together, as she would leave, I would hand her a used envelope, saying, "This is for your gasoline." At times I could only give her forty-six cents. I was embarrassed at the sum, but it was all I had to offer then.

One day, to my great surprise, she handed me a clean envelope. In it I found sixty-six dollars. She said that her Sunday school class had learned that even in my weakness I was serving the Lord by faith. They had baked and canned food to sell, and the proceeds were designated to help our work. This was the first time I ever received such a love gift. It truly encouraged me to continue working in the Lord's vineyard. However, I was more surprised and encouraged to receive the following lines from her own pen, after we had been working together for more than fifteen years:

A TRIBUTE TO MY QUEEN

Her chamber may seem very dark
When first you enter it,
But soon the Saviour's face you'll see
As by her side you sit.

I thank my Heavenly Father
For all to me she's meant—
For trials and for joys we've shared
Since I to her was sent.

In her I have seen patience,
Faith, contentment, love so true:

Of God she's asked again and again,
"What wilt Thou have me do?"

My prayer is that I may be
More like this one I love.
Won't it be just wonderful
To see her crowned above?

And so I beg, "Dear Father,
Be merciful and bless
Her remaining days and years
Just as Thou seest best."

Praise the Lord that all the time, as we have worked so closely, we have never had any harsh words or misunderstandings. Many times we have carried separate personal burdens that we could share with no one, not even each other. These could have disturbed our work for Him each time when we came together. But instead, we prayed and laid these burdens on the Lord and proceeded to work in harmony. Then we found we did not want to pick them up again. We left them with our burden Bearer, Jesus Christ.

Later on, the Lord miraculously brought to us a very talented Chinese friend to join us in serving Him. Grace Ng was the president of a Christian school for about twenty years in the Philippines. She had led her whole family to follow the Lord.

She is truly a woman of prayer. Very, very often long-distance phone calls come to ask her for prayer for difficult problems and for spiritual advice. Nothing can hinder her from spending an hour in prayer on her knees morning and evening. She longs for everyone who enters this house to know Jesus Christ and helps them to have a clear understanding of being born again.

For extra cleaning chores we have sometimes employed some traditional Amish women to help. They would arrive, promptly roll up the long black sleeves of their billowy dresses, and attack the most difficult tasks of scrubbing, polishing, and cleaning. They accomplished wonders 'with nonautomatic brooms, scrub pails, mops, and their own skillful hands. This helped me wonderfully because they worked so fast and silently, not jarring my sensitive ears with the whir of vacuum cleaners, but working with the quietness of well-seasoned muscles.

One day an Amish lady appeared, alighting from her carriage and tying her horse to our tree. She declared, "Miss Tsai, I just read your book and so I came to see you." After a most interesting conversation, she took from her pocket a well-worn small bag. She counted out her pennies one by one on my bed, fifty-six cents in all, and said, "Miss Tsai, I want to help you in your work." I never forgot her warm smile and sincerity.

For lighter, routine tasks of washing dishes, helping to get us settled for the night after our evening meal, and other work that should be done by younger legs, China Mary engaged neighborhood high school girls. Knowing that young high school girls often had school events cropping up at unexpected times, she hired several different girls to help us, teaching them each the same work. When we had extra guests, meetings, or health emergencies, she had a reservoir of help at her beck and call.

But her primary desire was that she might reach these young girls for the Lord. She often set aside some of their regular tasks to call them into her room, asking them to read some Bible passage to her, especially after her eyesight was failing. Sometimes it was to read an article from a Christian magazine, or to listen to a radio sermon, or to take home a

Christian record or cassette and later report to her about it. She invested her prayers and her time in these girls, believing that God's Word would not return void but in due season would come to harvest. We Chinese say, "The bamboo shoots all of a sudden spring up."

The Lord took China Mary to her heavenly home before some of the seed had sprouted. Later, one by one, five of them could hardly wait to come to tell me how Christ came into their hearts and how they longed for others to know Jesus and follow Him. Others told me how these girls had already influenced their parents, friends, relatives, and even a boyfriend. One of the girls wrote a tribute to China Mary:

"She was one of the most admired people that I have ever known. Her life was an example for every Christian, completely devoted to the Lord. I always felt that being with her each day was a new experience in Christ. Though I was a teenager and she was 92, her faith did not seem old to me because she renewed it every day of her life."

On some of the big occasions when our parlor overflowed with Chinese friends, officers, and students, I was aware that without our Christian friends from the community and churches, this would never have been possible. These friends have been like a treasure from the Lord. Not only have they worked with us, but they have encouraged me by their visits and letters.

FIFTEEN

Holiday Haven

Chinese students by the thousands are scattered in nearly all of the universities and colleges of this land, and at holiday time most of them do not get to go home as do their American classmates. Gradually, as they heard about us and "the little bit of China" that was in Paradise, many of them began to make our home their home on Thanksgiving, Christmas, Easter, and other holidays.

At Thanksgiving they learned how to roast and carve the traditional turkey and bake pumpkin pies and other goodies. More than that, they learned that the true meaning of the celebration is to give thanks and praise to God for their many blessings.

Christmas found the Chinese students decorating our rooms with colored lights and the Christmas tree with tinsel and bulbs. The girls put on their best Chinese dresses and the young men put on their ties to welcome group after group who came in to sing Christmas carols. They stood in a row to welcome them, bowing when they left. On Christmas Eve when carolers came from far and near, the students would hurry to turn on the floodlight at the doorway and invite them in to have a hot drink. Most of all, they learned that Christ who was born in a manger in Bethlehem had come into the world to bring salvation to all men.

One Easter I was asked to speak to a large group of stu-

Chinese students decorated our rooms for Christmas.

dents about Jesus' resurrection. A pretty young Chinese girl, a Ph.D. candidate, and daughter of a very wealthy Philippine businessman, suddenly exclaimed, "Why, I have been in this country for seven years, but just this morning the Holy Spirit convinced me that I need to confess before others that I am a sinner. I want to believe in Jesus and receive baptism!" Her baptism took place not long after, on a very quiet and beautiful Sunday afternoon. I was helped by two strong friends out of my darkened room to sit on the chaise lounge. It was the very first time I had left my room to participate in a service. I felt like Lazarus raised from the tomb!

After the message, China Mary accompanied the young lady to the front as she knelt to receive baptism. Her face was radiant. It seemed like a host of angels was worshipping Jesus and giving Him the glory because a lost sheep had been brought back to the fold. Her step took real courage because she would soon return to her unbelieving family to face much opposition. This was only the beginning of many more students, seamen, and military men accepting the Lord and being baptized in our home.

Our home was also the setting for the first Christian Chinese wedding in Lancaster County. Nearly two-hundred guests assembled in our parlor to attend the ceremony. China Mary had the floor structure and basement beams of our over 250-year-old house reinforced in anticipation of the large crowds now assembling regularly in our home. We usually borrowed folding chairs from the local funeral parlor to seat so many friends. Preceding the service an international quartet from Westminster College was sent as a special favor from the president of the school. Our local Presbyterian pastor officiated at the double-ring cremony in front of the palm-banked altar in our parlor.

The bride-to-be volunteered her recollections: "It was on Christmas 1949, the year that Miss Tsai and Miss Leaman returned from China, that I first visited the Leaman home. My mother had called on them in Shanghai and was impressed with their love and work. Because they were in such poor health, Mother urged that we go to visit them and give them any help we could. But over twenty-five years have passed since then and we haven't helped them one bit. On the contrary, we so often received their help and encouragement.

"During the time I was a student at Princeton, whenever there was a vacation, members of our family and friends took off for Paradise. In 1954 I met the man I was one day to marry. In January 1955 my fiancé accepted Christ right in the Leaman living room. We dedicated our lives to the Lord together. On February 19th of that year we were married in the Leaman home, with preparation and responsibility being cared for by these two elderly folk. A deep spiritual impression was left on each one who attended.

"As our three children came along, they were loved by these dear old folks as much as by their own grandparents. When we visited them, there were always toys for the children to play with. When they grew a bit bigger, there were candies on hand for them. After the children went to school, the dear folks read Bible story books to them and sent the books home as gifts. Afterward, when Miss Leaman's eyes became poor, she wrote her last letter to the children, urging them to love their parents and to lead others to the Lord. On our last visits, when she couldn't see at all, she still touched each one and called their names, sang with them, repeated Bible verses, and asked each one about his school. She told them when they went home to write and tell her all that they had seen on their excursion.

"When news reached us of Miss Leaman's home-call, the three children decided they must go to her memorial service and they volunteered a musical number. We had always gone to the Leaman home on festive occasions with gladness in our hearts. This time it was a funeral—but somehow still a festive occasion. It was the joyous celebration of a faithful child of God entering the gates of Heaven amid happy shouts of the angelic hosts! As we left the cemetery, our oldest said, 'I'm happy! At least we could do this much for Grandma!' None of us could be sad at her departure—not for her, only for us that we would miss her Christlike love and care for us."

SIXTEEN

Responses

I am a native-born Chinese. But I wrote my book in English. My Chinese friends gave me no peace until the Chinese translation was under way. The Chinese edition came out in 1955 and has become one of the best sellers.

One day I received a letter from a Chinese woman that revealed a story stranger than fiction. She had been a secretary for the Communists in China for six years. Eventually she escaped to Hong Kong. Lonely and depressed, she refused to have anything to do with church or Christianity. She would not read any Christian literature, and twice she was found just in time by her neighbors as she tried to commit suicide. A woman called on her and casually left a copy of my book on her bureau, hurrying off before it could be refused.

Still determined to end her life, she prepared a double dose of poison. When she was ready to take it, a voice seemed to say to her, "Read that book before you take the poison." She did. She read it through twice without stopping. Her terrible sins were revealed to her. Crawling on the floor, she sobbed for hours in repentance. Her letter said, "My doubts all disappeared. Before, this Jesus had seemed far away—just a myth. Suddenly He was very, very real. My heart brimmed over with unspeakable gratitude and I determined to accept Him as my Savior." She learned of my whereabouts through a church, and we carried on an extensive correspondence. Not only did she become an earnest Christian, but she also started a Bible class which later became a Christian church.

When the Communists occupied China they wanted to destroy every kind of religion, and that included the lamas. Temples were burned, idols destroyed, and lamas killed. Some tried to escape to India over the Himalaya Mountains. Most of these refugees died on this dangerous trip, although some got as far as the border of India. They were exhausted and their feet were one mass of blisters from climbing the rugged mountains.

At the foot of the Himalaya Mountains there is a little chapel of the Moravian Christian Church where some missionaries live. They came upon the lamas lying half-dead on the ground—a pitiful sight. They gave them water and food. A number of children among them were almost starved. The missionaries made an offer to the adults, saying, "We would like to help your children if you will permit us to feed them and teach them free."

Among the children was a certain seven-year-old. He was old enough by custom to enter the lama temple, and his mother had already determined that he should do so. But since he was starving to death and there was an opportunity for his life to be saved, the mother allowed him to go with the missionaries. At the age of eleven, this very bright boy, who studied well, decided to accept Christ as his Saviour. He learned to read the Indian language, and an Indian translation of my book came to his hands. The Holy Spirit evidently touched his heart. He thought, *When I finish my education, if the Lord would guide me, I would like to translate that book into the Tibetan language. Our people do not have books or literature to read except the religious books of*

They came upon the lamas lying half-dead on the ground.

the lamas and repeated prayers. He recalled seeing much Christian literature and Bibles in some homes. He longed for his people to have such books to read.

Another missionary managed to help the boy come to Canada to study in a Bible college. In his leisure time he actually translated my book into Tibetan. As I am writing this, I have just received a letter from him saying that he has finished it. He knew a friend in India who had a publishing house and wrote to him asking if he would consider publishing this book. The friend agreed to publish one thousand copies. He writes, "My people are poor. They don't have money to buy a book, so we may have to give it to them. Pray that the Lord will guide my people to read the book and accept Christ as you did."

One of the most touching reactions to the book was a letter from my own nephew in Taiwan. Woodrow grew up amid the scenes in my book. I trembled when I sent him one of the first copies. He is one of the few remaining Tsai relatives with whom I have any contact. He wrote,

> Your book just arrived. Congratulations, Auntie! It is beautiful—a beautiful name and so very beautifully written. I had an engagement last night, but before the dinner was finished, I thanked my host and came back home hurriedly to meet "the Queen." I went through your book in three hours. It is much richer than the luscious food I had! You must have received many flattering remarks from all your readers, but myself, "Ever-Cheer" in your book, knows you well from the inside, and is glad to verify that everything you mentioned in it is true and to the point. That is the important thing for any autobiography. You said you wrote it as if you were telling your story to a friend—I think rather that you have prepared a report to your Lord. The Lord will judge your achievement through all those you have led to believe in Him. You shall surely win the first prize!

One day I got a surpirse letter from Canada on stationery from the famous missionary-minded church, The Peoples Church in Toronto. It was from their noted pastor, Dr. Oswald J. Smith. Among other things, he wrote:

> So stirred was I to read your book that I was hardly able to lay it down when once I had started reading it. When I think of all that you have come through for Christ, I feel that I have done so little. He has undertaken for you in a marvelous way and you have been most faithful to Him. You have won many souls and you are assured of a crown. I think of your suffering and my heart goes out to you . . . . I want you to know that I have been praying definitely for you. Your book has given me a new understanding of Chinese life among the wealthy classes. I do so want to bring about a reconciliation between the people of China and the people of America. We and the Chinese ought to be the best of friends. Your book will help heal that wound. It will free us from prejudice against the Chinese. Our hatred of Communism has poisoned our minds and hearts toward these lovely people, who, when Jesus lives in their hearts, are unsurpassed for their simple, beautiful saintliness. In you we see them as they can be and as the noblest of them are . . . . Sometime ago I wrote a little poem for you to show you how greatly my heart was stirred by your story. Here it is:

I WANT YOU TO KNOW

I want you to know you are never forgotten,
The Savior is with you, He sees all your grief;
Remember, He cares, He will never forsake you,
And soon He is coming to bring you relief.

I think of you daily and pray for you always,
How often I see you in darkness and pain;

But though you must suffer, His grace is sufficient,
And someday with Jesus forever you'll reign.

The Lord will be with you, dear Queen of the darkness,
And all of earth's shadows will soon pass away;
For you have been faithful and many in Heaven
Will praise you for turning their darkness to day.

Your book has brought blessing, it makes me unworthy,
For you have accomplished so much by His grace;
Someday you will step from your chamber of darkness,
For Jesus remembers; you'll see His dear face!

With Christian affection, my sister from China,
I send you this message—your prayers He will hear;
I want you to know that God's mercy is o'er you—
Forgotten? No, never! Your Savior is near!

OSWALD J. SMITH

SEVENTEEN

Stupid Donkey

When Major Chang arrived from Taiwan at Aberdeen, Maryland, to learn the techniques of modern warfare at the Proving Grounds there, he realized that his English was inadequate to understand his classwork. An American officer's wife offered to tutor him. She used *Queen of the Dark Chamber* for a text. He soon realized it was written by a Chinese and when he learned that I lived within driving distance, he asked her, "Will you take me to meet this lady?"

Later he wrote about his visit to us in a Chinese magazine.

> I stepped into a dark chamber to meet Miss Tsai who had been bedridden for so many years. Forgetting my rank, I sat by her bed on a small kindergarten chair and chatted with her. Deep down in my heart I experienced a sudden upsurging of peace, joy and hope. Right there I was born again and really saved. From that time I have tried to live a real Christian life inspired by Miss Tsai, not because of her own strength, but by the Holy Spirit who spoke to my heart through her lips.

How God used this very first contact with the Chinese military to enlarge the circle of witness even to other shores.

Back at the base, he excitedly reported his visit to fellow Chinese officers. A week later, a consecrated Christian secretary at the Proving Grounds, Miss Edna Hill, who had also

116

read the book and wanted to meet us, drove over with five more Chinese officers. They were all high-ranking military personnel, carefully chosen for their exceptional qualifications. We sensed the importance of these contacts. Each man won for Christ could influence his own family and many men under him and they, in turn, could reach their relatives and friends. What a wonderful "army of the cross" that might be! Each officer won for Christ would be an important victory for the Lord of Hosts in His eternal war to save the world from sin and death. And as for us in this remote corner of rural America, it spelled opportunity—now we could still carry on our missionary work among the Chinese!

One copy of my book had started the ball rolling. These and subsequent groups of officers visited us time and again and invited their friends to come along. Faithful Edna Hill and others often brought them over in their cars. We urged them to think of our house as their home away from home and of us as their relatives here in America.

China Mary became "Great Aunt" to them and I, "Seventh Aunt." We always presented a Christian message, had prayer with them, and taught the Bible. We never insisted that they join a particular church. Each one who made a decision for Christ and asked for baptism did so of his own free will. After his baptism, each man wrote his own testimony of why he had believed. Then he made a tape recording of his experience and a prayer. In this way, other military men coming later could hear the testimonies of their fellow officers and be helped and blessed.

For years, almost every holiday and on many weekends, groups of two, three, four, or more officers came to our house to spend the day. Their course of military training would usually last only a few months, and the groups became much smaller. But each group visited us many times before they returned to Taiwan. They said, "Formosa [Taiwan] means 'Beautiful,' and we would be interested to see the beautiful things in America, too, but we prefer to come to you and find out what the Bible teaches." So they came every possible weekend. Nine different pastors baptized about seventy-two of these men through the fifteen years of this particular military program at Aberdeen.

What gives us the deepest satisfaction is the knowledge that many of these men have become missionaries to their own countrymen. Although the foreign missionaries have been withdrawn from the China mainland, these Chinese leaders are effectively ministering in His name. The army of the Lord for China is marching on!

God has given us a special respect for these brave men who are committed to the task of defending their country. We prayed that through us they would feel a certainty of an unseen Power above and beyond our own that was sustaining us, that they would find in us love transcending human affection, shining through clay, and that as a result they would find a faith in a heavenly Father more real than the material facts of existence. They had come here to learn how to use the most frightful weapons ever devised by man. They knew the indescribable horrors their use would let loose upon the world. And, more personal to them, they knew they were the ones who would train others to be sent to the front lines to be the first victims in any attack. They were being taught how to fight and how to kill, but not how to live or how to die. What they needed most was not a skill to fight, but a faith to live and to die for. They needed most of all to know the love of God.

Most of these officers were not battle-scarred veterans who had tasted blood, but youths torn from their families and forced to flee their native land. They were desperately lonely boys without their wives or children and only the barest pittance to live on. They knew the suffering of those back on the mainland of China, and yet they were helpless to deliver them. Only minutes away by plane across the straits of Taiwan were bombers that could pour down a rain of death. And entrenched on mainland China was the Red Army with its missiles trained on the island.

So to these men, the message of a heavenly Father who loved and watched over them, a gracious Lord who died for them, a Holy Spirit abiding forever in their hearts, a heavenly home awaiting them, and the exceedingly great and precious promises of God to comfort them in all their trials—this faith was able to melt their bitterness, relieve their frustrations, and fill them with joy. It also drew them together in a new brotherly fellowship. It set before them a better way of life, and gave them a cause worth dying for.

Just why did these colonels, majors, and captains of the Chinese army seek the society of four crippled old ladies like us? They summed it up in the term they so often used: warmth. Though they knew we were doing this for the Lord, they also knew we truly loved and understood them. They felt at home with us. It was as simple as that. Their intellectual attainments were far above ours, but they sat at my bedside and listened eagerly as I tried to introduce them to Christ. The simple illustrations made the deepest impressions. I tried to see things through their eyes, to show them what it meant to be "a soldier of the cross."

This work, though exhausting and demanding, was very sweet. I was glad I was old! Had I been young, I could never have done it. Because of my age they looked upon me as an aunt and treated me with the deference the Chinese so graciously accord their elders. But the pupils soon outstripped their teacher. They kept asking so many searching questions that I began to worry. The climax came when they said they wanted to come and study the Bible with me.

Me, a Bible teacher? Here was an opportunity but I felt unequal to the challenge. At night with tears I told my Lord, "I'm not a Bible teacher, and besides, I haven't been able to use my eyes for so many years. How can I teach them? I am just a stupid donkey!"

The Lord's answer was clear. "I used a donkey to speak to Balaam. I can use you!"

Praise His name, He did! He used this stupid donkey. When I met with the men to study God's Word, the Holy Spirit manifested Himself by taking control and teaching us together. Many friends also helped make this possible by their prayers and their loving service. The long, drawn-out, sustained effort for over fifteen years of those officers' contacts had drained our life's blood, but oh, the rewards!

EIGHTEEN

Before the Footlights

One night just before Chinese New Year, a colonel phoned to tell me that a special class of Chinese officers from Taiwan at the Proving Grounds said they wanted to call on me the next day to offer their New Year's greetings.

"Tomorrow?" I gasped. "How many?"

"About forty."

I covered the phone and held a whispered conversation with China Mary, who answered without hesitation, "They have offered to spend Chinese New Year with us. It is of the Lord. We can't refuse the honor. Tell them to come."

I resumed, "We will be delighted. Come early and spend the day with us."

These men had the same forlorn feeling as American GIs finding themselves stationed in a foreign land on Christmas Day. Away from everyone they loved and from every fond memory that made that season so dear, the officers were delighted to learn that there were four old ladies near Lancaster who understood what Chinese New Year meant to a Chinese.

I am sure it never occurred to them that they had presented us with an appalling task. We were to serve a New Year's feast, including two meals, to forty officers with twelve hours notice! They wouldn't ever think that it was an imposition! In China all heavy tasks are performed by well-trained servants, with the mistress of the family merely giv-

121

ing them orders and supervising their efforts. But here in
America we were four old cripples, dependent on the kindness and availability of others for even our basic needs. We
were living in a land where it is a tradition for every woman
to take pride in doing her own housework. Here no one
wants to be thought of as a servant. Modern conveniences
and ingenious gadgets are the servants available.

However, we had long since ceased to ask God why He
let people impose on our weaknesses or invade our privacy
at all kinds of inconvenient times. This anticipated day especially was an unparalleled honor and a marvelous opportunity that could not be lost, no matter what the cost.

"Oh, just give them hot dogs and ice cream," a friend
advised hoping to simplify the work. China Mary did not
answer but vanished to her cubbyhole office-bedroom. She
shut the door and began to make out a list of all the food we
would need. It was nearly ten o'clock when she picked up
the phone to rouse the storekeeper. She dared to ask him to
deliver everything we needed that very night. After all, the
next day was Sunday! Then she called the turkey farm for
huge turkeys and called the dairy for ice cream. She had
decided it was going to be a real New Year's feast with all the
trimmings!

Even at that late hour I phoned some other friends to
come and help us entertain. One exclaimed incredulously,
"You can't be serious! You can't possibly do it. This doesn't
make sense!" No, it didn't make sense, but it was for Christ.
I phoned another Christian Chinese friend in New Jersey.
She answered cheerfully, "We just got back from Chinatown
and bought all kinds of Chinese food. I won't need to sleep
tonight. It is Chinese New Year's eve, anyway, and I am
going to start cooking right away! I'll come early tomorrow
morning."

Despite their misgivings, our friends rallied loyally. In addition to the feast, we had to arrange for a Christian service. Since most of the officers knew little or no English, we had to find a leader who could speak Chinese. Next we called on our neighbors, asking them to help prepare and serve the feast and, of course, to wash the anticipated piles of dishes! Fortunately the Leamans had cupboards and cupboards of beautiful dishes inherited from earlier generations. The neighbors not only agreed to come, but they also contributed large dishes of delicacies which they had hurriedly prepared. Besides all this, we invited interested friends from as far away as Philadelphia. We wanted them to join the party and meet our Chinese guests. Two other essential jobs were to charter a bus to convey the officers and to borrow folding chairs for the service.

It was well after midnight when we turned off the lights and tried to sleep. We had burned the telephone wires, roused sleepy people out of bed, and answered a chorus of incredulous whats, whys, and hows. Even that night the table was already set and preparations under way. The next day we didn't serve five thousand, but we did serve over one hundred, and not for one meal but two!

When the bus rolled into our yard, the driver found it already full of parked cars. When he opened the bus door, colonels, majors, captains, and lieutenants all trooped out in their natty olive drab uniforms and proud insignia. Bowing and smiling with caps in hand, they entered our humble home. They were not stiff and formal, though they observed strict military protocol among themselves. To us they were more like a lot of boys who were home on leave. They greeted us like old friends. Some were from Hunan, some from Peking, others from Shanghai and many other places. Each spoke his own peculiar dialect of Chinese, which only

Bowing and smiling with caps in hand, they entered our humble home.

the experienced ear can differentiate. Some were veterans of the war with Japan, but most were young men who had fled Communist China and had joined the army on Formosa.

The table was laden with a typical American turkey dinner. We couldn't provide a Chinese feast out of a magic hat on such short notice. But still there were ample Chinese foods and the typical Chinese New Year's array of fruits, nuts, dates, cakes, and other delicacies. Each signified a traditional New Year's wish for happiness, long life, health, prosperity, many sons, family unity, and so forth. China Mary explained the Christian symbolism of each item, and because it came from such a motherly person, they enjoyed her injunction to be "the heavenly Father's good, obedient boys." Later, before a large group of friends, the colonel said, "I know how to order my ten thousand soldiers to obey me. Now I want to learn to obey my heavenly Father's order."

Our big house was crowded to capacity with guests and volunteer workers, who almost stepped on each other's toes as they elbowed their way through the crowd. The officers were tremendously impressed with this display of Christian love and hospitality. This was Christianity in action, and they appreciated seeing the ladies hurrying around to give their time and service for Christ's sake. When they sat down to eat, personal evangelism started. Each Christian, with his or her tray, sat beside an officer to be friends and to share his faith. One of our friends presented each officer with a copy of *Queen of the Dark Chamber,* and the Gideons gave them each a New Testament.

After the service, with only one exception, they all held up their hands to signify their desire to believe in Jesus. At first I did not put much stock in this public expression, thinking it might only be a courteous gesture on their part in return for our hospitality. Only a few had any previous knowledge of Christianity. But later their commanding officer, a Christian, handed me a long list of those who had voluntarily signed their names, declaring their sincere desire to accept Christ. We did not see many of these men again, but some have written from Taiwan and have told me they now go to church. Some take their families with them, and some have actually joined a church. I know that the Spirit of God was present at our party. It was He who spoke to many on that New Year's Day.

"How do you know that those who say they accept the Lord in your dark chamber are really saved?" friends sometimes ask. This is never for me to judge. I am only to be faithful in proclaiming Christ to them. Let me share an example with you.

In China in 1919 when I started to serve the Lord by faith, I wrote articles for Chinese magazines and for a daily newspaper. A Miss Chen was my able Chinese secretary. But no matter how much I witnessed to her about Christ, she refused to believe in Him.

Once when I went to Pei-ta-ho for a conference, she secretly ran off to Shanghai and put an advertisement for a husband in the newspaper. A man answered and before long they were married. She gave him all her worldly possessions. On their honeymoon he took her to a famous place called Ging-san in Chin Kiang. In a secluded spot, he put his arms around her and said, "Look at this beautiful river." While they gazed at it, he violently pushed her into the river. She lived to later tell me this story.

As she was nearly drowning in the water, unable to swim, her whole past seemed to come before her. She remembered my witness about Christ and His willingness to save any sinner. She made a dying decision to accept Christ, though at the same time she was shrieking, "Revenge! Revenge!" As she was going down for the third time and at death's very door, men in a fishing boat suddenly saw her and she was quickly rescued. Nearly dead, she could not talk but made signs that she wanted to write. She gave the name and address of a certain hotel, writing that her husband of three days had attempted to murder her. Policemen were sent to the hotel and found him frantically moving out all his belongings. They arrested him on the spot. When Miss Chen was asked to testify in court against him, because of Christ newly in her heart, she reversed her attitude of vengeance. She stated before the court that because God had forgiven her sins, she would forgive this scoundrel. All she asked was that he return everything she had given him. This experience was the turning point in her life. From that moment she lived wholly for the Lord.

How do any of us know if a person is saved when his lips confess Christ? How do we know but that through our witness he will someday in the future come to Christ? If my secretary had drowned, of course she would have belonged to Christ. But to this day I would not have known that in her dying moment, like the thief on the cross, she had accepted Him. We must faithfully sow the seed of His Word in the Spirit and leave the results in His hand.

Expenses ran high for the fifteen or sixteen years that our opportunity with the officers was at its peak. One night as I was thinking and praying about this, I remembered a Christian man who headed a large corporation. Only once had he called on me. I decided to write him a letter, asking him if he would like to have a share in financing this work.

As I polished up the letter, I suddenly felt a restraint from the Lord. "Since 1919 you have served Me by faith," the Lord reminded me. "Do you want to beg now? This is My work. I will take care of it." Puzzled, but obedient, I tore up the letter. Again I was tempted to write him as bills piled up. Five times I wrote and five times I tore up the letters. "Daughter, sit still," the Lord assured.

A few months later, I was surprised to receive a letter from this same gentleman. He said, "From reading different periodicals, and from friends who have been helping in your work with the Chinese officers, I have come to see the value of your ministry. I have decided to have a little financial share."

In reply, to express our appreciation for how the Lord had moved his heart, I told him about the five letters that I had written to him and destroyed. He answered that this showed to him the Lord's seal of approval on his decision to help our work. But he went on to say that if I had mailed those letters, he would not have been able to give to the work. He asked me to make a bargain with him. I was to tell no one except Miss Leaman that he was contributing to our ministry. If I did, he would not be able to continue it.

As the work expanded, this gentleman suggested to China Mary and me that we incorporate our work so that others could contribute to it with tax benefits. We backed away from such a complication. We knew it would involve at least a secretary, treasurer, office work, and much red tape of accountability to the government and public. "I will pay for your accountant and secretary," he offered.

But we declared, "We really have no 'work.' God only brings us opportunities which come and go according to His good pleasure." This kind friend was summoned to his heavenly home just four months before China Mary.

NINETEEN

Ministry Multiplies

One December afternoon, three Chinese officers enroute to the West Coast gazed spellbound from the windows of their express train. It sped away, leaving the wintry Lancaster County landscape behind in the glowing sunset. For a moment the train clicked along the shining railway tracks winding between the long, clean lines of modern factories, then for a few miles it paralleled a busy highway bordered with neat rows of cottages screened behind the bare branches of maples. Next it roared through the stillness of rolling fields dotted with dazzling white clusters of farmhouses, with here and there a slender church spire piercing the sky.

"What a beautiful, happy corner of the earth! Lancaster, we are proud of you, we will always bless you!" one of them murmured.

"Yesterday we said good-by to Great Aunt [Mary Leaman] and Seventh Aunt [me]. Two weeks ago we were baptized in their home. Today we are on our way back to Taiwan. What a change these few weeks have brought!" said another man. "We will never be the same."

"Even a heart of steel would have melted at that parting yesterday," said the third man. "I still feel the glow of God's love filling my heart."

"I have an idea," the first man said. "Let's each write a poem to Great Aunt and Seventh Aunt and ask them to

129

translate the verses into English for our American friends to read."

"Splendid!" they all agreed. So each took out pencil and paper and began composing what they called "free lines." In China, when friends part, "like the morning and evening star, never to meet again," it is a time-honored custom to exchange poems rather than letters. Here are the three poems they sent us, translated freely:

Lieutenant Colonel H. wrote:

Lancaster,* you are a beautiful, bountiful, wonderful land!
Churches, farms and factories glitter on your breast like medals!
Even a passing stranger would be deeply impressed,
How much more we who came and went so often!
Here is an open-handed, open-hearted Meng-Chang!†
Here is mankind's most perfect, friendly warmth!
Although we come from a far distant land,
To be here is like returning home.

Here is a bridge leading to Heaven,
Ah, Heaven, Heaven we can see with our own eyes,
Not one a million miles away!

For you, friends, who live in this happy corner of earth,
We reverently and sincerely pray.
May God give you joy and preserve your bodies and souls forever.

Today we are parted for a while.
Yet at some future day we will joyfully meet again.
Lancaster, we will always praise you.
Lancaster, we will always bless you.

---

*By "Lancaster" they meant to refer to Leaman Place, Paradise, Pennsylvania, and their associations with us.

†Meng-chang is known in Chinese history for his lavish hospitality. He is said to have entertained as many as one hundred guests at a time, many of whom were persons of distinction. His home was surrounded by trees, but he loved his guests so much he couldn't bear to have them go, and so he cut down the trees in order to watch them until they were out of sight.

Lieutenant Colonel T. wrote:

Lancaster, the spot where people love to linger!
Here are kind hearts and friendly homes
That have entertained many officers from China.
These days though few and brief in time
Have wrought a change in our lives so great
They'll never be forgotten.

We were a flock of lost sheep
But we have found shelter in the Shepherd's fold;
The angel of the Lord beckoned us
To leave darkness and be born again.
We want to share in the joy of those kind old people there!

Ah, Great Aunt and Seventh Aunt, how kind and good you are,
May God give you happiness, long life and peace!
His the power to bestow, His the dominion forever and ever.
Lancaster, we are proud of you,
Lancaster, we will spread abroad your fame.

Major L. wrote:

Lancaster, you are our heaven on earth.
You hold the keys of Jesus Christ to open our closed and
    locked hearts.
Let us enjoy this heavenly place together,
May we never, never, NEVER forget each other!

May this parting be but for a while,
Our hearts o'er flow with children's love and devotion.
God, bind our hearts together,
God, cause these few kind old people
To live forever in that heaven on earth!

Ah, Lancaster, you are the place where I was born again.
I'll remember you, I'll keep you always in my heart
So I may ever behold those rays of heavenly light.

I want to imitate you, I want to take the keys of God
To the four corners of the earth,
To open ten thousand times ten thousand hearts
That are still locked and sealed in darkness.

When Colonel Peter walked into my room, he had already rehearsed his lines well. He stood straight and proud and declared, "I am from Taiwan. I heard from Colonel B. what a remarkable woman you are. I have come to visit you. But I am an atheist. I don't believe in Christianity. You can never make a Christian out of me!"

With such an introduction, no words I could have prepared would have reached his heart. I prayed silently, then asked him, "Did you come directly from Taiwan?"

"Yes."

"What did you eat for breakfast?"

He replied, "Rice."

"And what for lunch?"

"Rice."

"And for supper?"

He replied impatiently, "You are a Chinese. You know we always eat rice!"

I asked, "Don't you get tired of eating rice three times a day?"

"Of course not! If we got tired of eating rice we would be sick!"

This gave me an opportunity, and I said, "I am a Christian. If I did not talk about Jesus, the bread of life, I would be sick!" He laughed, and the ice was broken. I knew the Holy Spirit could now go on to do His work. And He did!

Recording his testimony later, Colonel Peter confessed,

Not only had I not believed in Jesus, but had never given a thought about whether I would go to heaven when I died. My only hope was that in this life I could do something to serve my country and be a dutiful citizen. I used the strength and energy and wisdom that God gave me, but I never thought of obeying His command to serve Him. I was aimless and ignorant, just lost sheep, unable to direct my own steps, not knowing whether to turn to the east or to the west.

Not until my third visit to America did I meet Great Aunt and Seventh Aunt, two of God's kindly old people. All the time they talked about salvation and the love of Jesus, things I had never heard about before. It was a revelation to me and caused my darkened heart to turn to the light. For the first time, I knew that I was a sinner, that I had only thought about my own way and never asked God's guidance. No wonder I went astray and failed to find happiness. These two old people are certainly God's "hunting dogs" who brought me into His sheepfold. I accepted Christ in Leaman Place and was baptized. From then on, my heart has been filled with joy. "Look unto Jesus, exalt Him and be faithful until death" is my motto.

Two Chinese colonels, a Muslim and an atheist, were among those sent to Aberdeen for training. After finding out about us, they came to our home every possible weekend, although motivated mostly by a desire for fellowship with their own countrymen. Gradually the Lord began to touch their hearts and they became more open to His Spirit. They asked to come and study the Word of God with us on as many weekends as we could spare.

I helped arrange for them to go to a Billy Graham crusade in New York. When they returned they rushed to my room, asking, "Seventh Aunt, please explain to us what this Billy Graham means by 'believe, repent, and be born again.' " I was thrilled to be able to point them to Christ.

When the officers' work first started, China Mary wrote to a friend,

To think that right here in our old homestead, right where
my father was born over a hundred years ago, here where as a
child he heard people praying for an open door to China, here
where he said good-bye to home and loved ones more than
eighty years ago to spend a lifetime of missionary service in
China, here, now that China Mainland's doors are again
closed, the Lord, in His matchless grace and loving kindness is
sending Chinese officers of the Free China army to hear the
gospel!

The opportunity never ceased to amaze us!

Some American friends wonder at the emphasis that we
and the new converts put on the rite of baptism after persons have made decisions to accept Christ. It is not that we
believe baptism is essential for salvation. It is an outward sign
of what has already happened in their spirits—they have
passed from eternal death to the gift of eternal life. But
coming from an Oriental background, the outward sign of
baptism is a serious expression for all the world to see. The
new believer declares that he has made a once-for-all
commitment—a clear confession to follow Christ. It has almost the same importance as a wedding ceremony, "For-
saking all others, I cleave unto Him alone." That is why so
many of those who finally made decisions for Christ immediately thought of being baptized to give expression to
their new faith. In their hearts they meant, *No turning back.
I give myself without reserve to my Saviour and Lord.* Baptism for repentance of sins is taught in the Scripture. We do
not insist on any specific manner of administering the baptism, but leave it to the convictions of each believer as he
interprets it for himself from Scripture.

We always regarded follow-up work for the officers returning to Taiwan as urgent. I often counseled them, "You received Christ in America. You may think that after you re-

turn home nobody will know what you do there. So your 'fox tail' might come out in your home. You may have a bad temper or treat your family unkindly. You must pray to Jesus to help you be a real Christian right in your home, which may be the hardest place to live for Him."

Praise the Lord! We heard that thirteen families of those converted officers were brought to the Lord in Formosa. The one whom God used was a beloved pastor, Dr. Chen Wei-Ping. He wrote us by his own hand at the age of ninety-three, "In spite of being advanced in age, I am still preaching the gospel. I am closely associated with the officers who came to the Lord at Leaman Place. Your works are permanent and glorious."

As further follow-up, we sent the officers subscriptions to Christian magazines, introduced them to Christians abroad, and even tried to find Christian wives for some of them. Now every Christmas we receive a beautiful array of greeting cards which I string up in my room.

I wrote to President and Madame Chiang Kai-shek in Taiwan, enclosing a copy of my book and telling about these men who had confessed Christ. Madame Chiang sent me the following letter:

OFFICE OF THE PRESIDENT
REPUBLIC OF CHINA

Taipei, Taiwan
May 1956

Dear Miss Tsai:

It was good of you and Miss Leaman to entertain so many of our officers from Aberdeen. I am sure it meant a great deal to them to be in a home during their first lonely days in America. Through our prayer groups our chaplains who

Chinese seamen are welcomed by friends from Paradise.

work with the armed forces can be informed about these officers who become Christians while in America so that they will progress in their spiritual life when they return.

With all good wishes,

Yours sincerely,

May-ling Soong Chiang

(Madame Chiang Kai-Shek)

Many Chinese cargo boats come from Taiwan to Philadelphia and Baltimore. Faithful Yun Yong, who started the seamen's work, kindly brought seamen to see me from time to time. Reverend Maynard Lu shepherded the seamen diligently and ministered to them and their families in Baltimore. Over the years we had the privilege to witness to them. A number of them received baptism in our home, and many were baptized on the boat and other places.

These Christian seamen planned all kinds of ways to lead other seamen and their families to follow the Lord. They held a weekly service on the boat for those who had not believed, they collected good Chinese books for the seamen, and they made brass boxes for collections, not only to help in the seamen's work, but also for mission work.

A Captain Shih accepted the Lord in my dark chamber. He led his chief engineer, some officers, many crewmen, and his wife to believe and to receive baptism.

Within a week, three Chinese captains of cargo boats either called on me in person or by telephone. Captain C. encouraged me by saying, "Seven years ago I was in your home and had my picture taken with Miss China Mary Leaman in your sitting room. The Lord spoke through both of you. My heart was very much touched and I became a Christian. I am sending you my tiny offering for the Lord's work. I am really a debtor to you for your spiritual help. I will try to come to see you when my boat returns to America."

This helped me realize that when we follow the Lord's direction in sowing the seed, we should trust the Holy Spirit to water it and give the increase. We may not see any result, but we should not be disappointed. If we *do* see results, it may be because someone else sowed the seed years ago and God gave us the privilege of reaping.

TWENTY

Understudies

The thousands of Chinese students in America and Canada have been much in our hearts, prayers, and ministry. "But at your advanced age, how can you relate to today's young people?" I have often been asked. "Don't you feel some kind of generation gap?"

Not at all, I'm happy to say! Chronological age has little to do with it.

The Chinese students come from Taiwan, Hong Kong, and other places in Southeast Asia, seeking the knowledge of this world in universities and colleges from coast to coast. Some were born on the China mainland and fled with their parents from the oppressors. A great many are professing Christians, children of Christian Chinese families, the fruit of faithful missionary labor. But some of their loving Christian parents have hesitated to allow their children to study in the United States. The stories they have heard and read about the godless university campuses, with riots, drugs, violence, and loose living make them fearful. But God's Spirit continues to hover over these Christian Chinese students in a very special way and is preserving them for purposes of His own "in the midst of a crooked and perverse nation" (Philippians 2:15).

Several special ministries, such as Ambassadors for Christ, Inc., Chinese Christian Mission, and others have been burdened with the spiritual welfare of Chinese students, and the Lord has used them fruitfully in America in the last couple of decades. He has given them a great field to work in. They have had the vision of evangelizing and building up the faith of the Chinese students in this land so they will not only stand firm for Christ, but also return to their homelands to witness for Him.

The circles these ministries have started continue to widen. They have established Chinese Bible study groups on college campuses, published Christian Chinese literature especially for the intellectuals, initiated missionary outreach by Chinese, and organized Christian retreats and conferences. They are pleasing the Lord by shepherding the Chinese students in this country. How happy we have been to have a part!

Much of our ministry in China was with students. As a young convert, while a student myself, I knew well the problems of fellow students. I was invited from school to school to speak to crowds of students about Christ. I usually spoke to non-Christians when I was associated with Miss Ruth Paxson, and she spoke to the Christians. I remember that some of the Christian students in True Light Middle School in Canton, China, went to the servants who worked in the school, urging them to come to my meetings. To make sure that the servants came to hear the gospel, they did their work during the meetings. After a few days, nearly every one of the servants accepted the Lord. How happy it made those girls!

In the early days of Christianity in China it was considered a very great success to persuade any girl or woman to accept a Bible. Later, girls and women were willing even to go without a new dress or other luxuries to wear at Chinese New Year, in order to save enough money to buy a Bible. We always encouraged them to purchase their Bibles rather than to accept those distributed freely. We found that when they paid for them, they valued them greatly. Of course, many of the girls in our Bible study classes had to buy their Bibles on the installment plan! Their families did not want them to have a Bible and often would not give them money for that purpose. The girls and women would come to class with red or green paper covers or some newspaper covering the Bibles in their hands. They loved them! Before they went home they usually wrapped up their Bibles carefully in their handkerchiefs so they would be protected during their walk home.

I rely heavily on the Lord Jesus Christ and His Word, the Bible, when I deal with the students who come to my bedside. I cannot possibly approach them on the same level as their academic training. It would be out of my field. Besides, the Christian life is not founded upon the intellect, but upon the response of the heart to the Holy Spirit's dealings. The Bible must be the basis.

"But do you understand every word of the Bible? Do you know the whole thing?" I have been asked. Of course I do not. The Bible has sixty-six books and I can't say that I understand the whole Bible. But I can say that the Bible understands me and knows me. Here is an illustration which has helped me understand about the Bible:

My parents had twenty-four children: my father's first wife bore him seven before she died, my mother fifteen, and a concubine had two children. In all, there were thirteen girls and eleven boys. Father was given a beautiful safe made in London, with twenty-six letters in the combination. Under the letter *U,* when my mother put in the key, it began to "sing"; when it stopped, the door opened automatically.

According to Chinese custom, at Chinese New Year, Dragon Festival, Full Moon Festival, and Father's and Mother's

"Whatever is inside belongs to you."

birthdays, all the children would wear new outfits. The girls put on pearl flowers, rings, bracelets, and other jewelry. Mother opened the safe only at night when the children went to bed. Then the next morning she would give the jewelry to us, saying, "You wear this or that." In the evening we would have to return it all to Mother. After we went to bed, Mother put the things back in the safe. I never questioned why Mother never allowed us girls even to see what was inside the safe.

Years went by and all my brothers and sisters were married. I was left alone with my mother. I remember very clearly one afternoon when she and I were alone, she suddenly put the key to the safe in my hand. "Daughter, you keep it," she said.

I did not know why. She went on, "All your brothers and sisters are married, and you alone are left with me. Open the safe. Whatever is inside belongs to you." No one could ever understand how I felt at that moment. I held the key in my hand reverently, trembling. I had never seen the inside of the safe, nor had I questioned my mother's love for withholding it. Suddenly I had the key to open it!

The Holy Spirit revealed to me a deep truth which helped me very much. The Bible, surely more important than this safe, and all the jewels inside the Bible are very precious. Some things we do understand, many things we don't, Deuteronomy 29:29 tells us. It taught me that when we read God's Word, we must never doubt or question our heavenly Father's love. Some things we must just wait to understand. Like the safe full of jewels, the day finally came when Mother could trust me with the key. We must never doubt the Bible or question its teachings. When the Lord's time comes, He will reveal to us the particular truth from the Bible that He wants us to know. We may read one verse dozens of times. We know the words but we cannot grasp the real meaning for ourselves. One day the interpretation or application suddenly leaps out at us. How happy we are! That verse then becomes a living word in our hearts.

The Bible has lots of jewelry inside. We Christians must trust our Father in heaven. I believe that every word is inspired by the Holy Spirit, even though I don't understand the whole Bible yet. I share this especially with students. Moody and Spurgeon knew much about the Bible and trusted it, so God revealed much of it to them. So He will reveal it to us as His trusting children.

The day after Christmas one year we had several Chinese houseguests whom we had entertained over Christmas. That morning when the mail was delivered, I received a package from a very kind friend whom I had met only twice. As our guests were preparing to leave, I put aside the package to devote myself to them. In the evening after these friends had gone, I rested on my pillows and let my thoughts fly back to my loved ones and friends in China. I wondered whether we would ever meet again in this world. While my thoughts roamed far and wide, my eyes fell upon my neglected package and I hurried to open it. Inside I found a box of writing paper, delicately scented and bearing the imprint of roses. There was a Scripture text on every sheet. Also enclosed were several airmail envelopes and even a sheet of stamps. How thoughtful! I was pleased by the paper's lovely scent and delicate appearance. Before putting away the box, I felt enticed to count the sheets of paper to see how many letters I could write. This was something I never bothered to do before. How surprised I was to find several crisp, new dollar bills between the pages! Immediately I was reminded of God's Book. Between its pages and in every line are hidden treasures. But alas! How often I neglect the Book; how much of the treasure I fail to gather up!

Sometimes students have come to me in groups. For about eighteen years, Chinese students from an annual summer conference sponsored by Ambassadors for Christ, Inc., have come to visit us each June. Sometimes I feel as if I am looking into a sea of faces as they crowd into my dark chamber. What can I share with these young intellectuals who are studying space physics, mathematics, engineering, philosophy, or medicine? I, who never finished college! Yet I am so amazed that time after time students have lingered, tears in their eyes, touched as the Holy Spirit illuminated some bit of truth that He led me to share with them. I still receive many letters from Chinese students who were moved through reading my book. God seems to use my background of Chinese education and family status to give this humble vessel a hearing with these young intellectuals. May He alone receive the glory! At times I have had a Ph.D. kneeling at my bedside or sitting in the kindergarten chair beside me. In God's sight, we are all His children, learning in His school. Sometimes we think we are ready for graduation, and then we find we need to go back to kindergarten to learn some elementary lesson.

One of the often repeated lessons I have learned from the Lord in my school of suffering is that when I have come to the absolute end of my strength, I can rest in the Lord and trust Him to use me. Every few weeks I must take medicine for the malaria that flares in my bone marrow. This medicine is very toxic and makes me feel so ill that it is impossible for me to talk to visitors. I am just unable to think or concentrate.

One day just after taking this medicine, when I was hardly able to raise my head, China Mary suddenly appeared to report that a busload of Chinese students from one of the conferences had arrived to visit me. In a daze, I murmured that it was impossible to see them. She knew it well, but she said that they would be very disappointed if they could not just come in and say hello before going on their way. I weakly consented, wondering how I could even open my eyes. Then I remembered that evangelist Billy Graham had said that wherever he went, people recognized him and wanted to speak to him, so he always tried to make himself available. My spirit was willing but my flesh was weak—I did not even feel physically available!

China Mary and Grace Ng, my co-worker, directed the group to my room and went out to the kitchen to prepare some refreshments. I still have no idea what I said because my mind was not clear. I remotely remember something about "commit" and "rest."

With the group was a brilliant Chinese professor, Dr. Lit-Sen Chang, who was a well-known writer on philosophy and theology and special lecturer in missions at a divinity school. He had held a high official position with the Chinese government before the Lord saved him. As he was leaving, he grasped my hand warmly and said, "It was not you who was speaking today, but the Holy Spirit!"

Soon I was startled to hear loud cries coming from the sitting room. Pheobe Chua, who had come from Manila that morning was resting upstairs, but when she heard the cries, she stumbled down the stairs and rushed into my room, certain that I was passing away! It turned out to be some students weeping because Professor Chang humbly testified to them that he had seen a sick person able to speak in the strength of the Holy Spirit. Although he was a theology teacher and the author of many books, that day he had been convicted of serving the Lord in his own strength and wisdom. His witness caused many to realize how much they also had failed to trust the Lord, and they sobbed with him, promising the Lord that from henceforth they would rely on the Holy Spirit. Then they all prayed and cried again. It truly proved the motto that hangs on the wall of my dark chamber, "Not I, but Christ!"

Our Sunday morning quiet in the Leaman home was shattered by the jangle of the phone one winter day. It was a friend who had received a long-distance call from New York City.

"There are two Chinese students from Canada coming on the bus this evening. They want to see you tomorrow," she announced. "I told them you had not been well and it was a risk to come without an appointment, but I could not convince them. They declared, 'We'll take our chances—we *must* see her!' "

I had been feeling especially weak and ill, and the doctor had cautioned me that I should see no one. I felt there was no way that I could see these men. "Tell them really not to come," I instructed my friend.

"I can't. They were in a phone booth in the station, had their tickets, and were about to get on the bus!"

I sighed, resigning myself to an ordeal that would surely overtax my strength. Then I remembered again China Mary's watchword: "restful availability" to whatever the Lord planned for our day. "If God sends someone, we must receive him from Him" was her motto, even when she was nearly exhausted. *There must be some special purpose for the coming of these young men,* I thought to myself, and called my co-workers in to pray with me about it.

"Here we are!" announced a voice on the phone at 8 P.M. that cold winter night. "We are along the highway in Paradise where the bus dropped us off." Our friends picked

them up, discovering that they were very young Chinese
university students from Canada. They were dressed in hik-
ing togs and boots, with bedrolls and knapsacks on their
backs. They looked for all the world like Canadian
woodsmen, except for their beaming Chinese faces.

They stayed overnight with our friends, warming themselves before the fireplace and consuming large quantities of
Chinese noodles after our friends discovered that they had
been trying to save money and had not eaten all day. But
they soon came to the point.

"We have waited six months to visit the 'Queen of the
Dark Chamber.' We spent all our money to make this trip
during our vacation and barely have enough to get back.
Our visas to re-enter Canada expire in two days, and we have
to hurry back or else we will lose our immigration status. Tell
us, what is the queen like? Do you have a photo? We are so
excited to see her that we shall not be able to sleep all
night!"

When our friends produced a photo, they passed it back
and forth laughingly, nervous with anticipation. "Now that
the time has come, we are almost afraid to go and see her!"
one of them said.

"Actually, for what purpose did you want to see Miss
Tsai?" our friends inquired.

"We really don't know," they said, shaking their heads.
"We only know that we were supposed to come. God must
have brought us." The next morning they were up with the
dawn. "Today is the day!" they said as they hurried through
breakfast.

When they walked into my room, I wondered why such
handsome young men would want to see an old invalid lady
who could be their great-grandmother. As soon as they introduced themselves, I made a short prayer with them, ask-

ing Jesus to guide our conversation that His name might be exalted. Then I asked them what made them come such a long way to see me. They explained that they had heard my name mentioned by their friends so often that it made them determined to come and see me for themselves.

I shared with them Philippians 3:8 in the Chinese translation: " 'I count it the most important thing *to know Christ.*' My name is not important," I told them. " 'As for man, his days are as grass,' " I reminded them from Psalm 103:15. "We Chinese always ask a person first of all, 'What is your name?' But even our names are not important. We will be given new names in heaven, according to Revelation 2:17. Even famous and important people may fail you. But the most important thing is to know Jesus Christ. He will never disappoint you. He is the only One who can satisfy you. He can help you solve all your problems and difficulties."

I told them this illustration: "Once a rich man had a tea party. A famous actor was asked to dramatize Psalm 23. There was loud applause at his talent. Then the host asked an old pastor to act out Psalm 23. He stood up and read it from the Bible slowly, reverently, and with meaning. Everything was quiet. No applause. The actor went over to the pastor with tears in his eyes and said, 'I know the words of Psalm 23 but you know the Shepherd.' "

I told those boys how honored I was for them to come so far to see me, but the best thing was for them to know Jesus.

"How was your visit?" the young men were asked as they flung their packs once more to their shoulders, preparing to return that night by train to Canada.

They were too choked with emotion to reply immediately. "I wept to leave her!" the older finally offered unashamedly.

"God talked to us through her," the other added. "She talked to us as if she were as young as we—like our sister, or friend. And yet she advised and taught us like a mother and a revered grandmother. We will never forget this day. Our lives are changed!''

TWENTY-ONE

Cameras Roll

For many years I had placed the idea of my story being made into a movie on God's altar if it would please Him. Not long after, Dr. Micah Leo, a Christian Chinese writer, put my story into dramatic form. Meanwhile, the Chinese Christian Mission had a burden from the Lord to make their first gospel movie in Chinese to reach the unchurched masses. They had no previous movie-making experience, no equipment, no actors, no professional staff or producer—only the vision to serve God. They approached me as to whether I would be willing for my book to be their first attempt at a Christian movie. After much prayer, I believed that the Lord was leading me to approve. Dr. William Culbertson, president of Moody Bible Institute, visited me one morning and agreed that a gospel movie was the thing to do.

A member of the staff of the Chinese Christian Mission, Andrew Ho, had been a radio singer in Taiwan for seventeen years and knew many people. He began to contact pastors and other Christians to enlist their prayers and help. They found Christians willing to learn the parts, regardless of whether they had acting experience or not. To my knowledge, few, if any, of them were professionals. They were simply believers in the Lord who wanted to serve Him. The drama by Dr. Leo was adapted into an abbreviated movie

151

script, and the project was launched with many prayers and an empty budget. Through many hardships, it was filmed on location in Taiwan. I do not appear in the movie myself. The soundtrack was in Chinese, the Mandarin dialect, with English subtitles. Later it was dubbed in English. It ran about an hour. This Christian mission had done its best for the Lord with its first venture, an amateur production. Indeed, the spiritual results from the showing of this humble film were as the water turned into wine by the Lord Jesus. Because He stoops to use "the weak things of the world to confound the things which are mighty" (1 Corinthians 1:27), it is the Lord and not men who receives the glory. In the written reports by the mission that made the film, it was stated,

> Our first gospel film in Asia, "Queen of the Dark Chamber," brought an enormous response. During the first few months there were seventy-two showings to 11,092 people, and 606 decisions for Christ were made, and 778 Christians dedicated their lives to serve the Lord. Many who otherwise would never have attended church have been reached. Others who had long been absent were challenged. Drama and film are indeed effective tools in reaching out to the unchurched people.

In the same issue, Jonathan Cheung stated his impression of the film:

> After watching the "Queen" film, we can clearly see three unreliable things: fame, status, wealth. We also see the three most crucial trials Christiana Tsai went through after she believed in the Lord: persecution by her family, desertion of her loved one and the loss of health. Yes, but she said, "I have had the Lord Jesus Christ as my Saviour." She lost her companion, but she gained an everlasting, ever-abiding friend. She lost her health, but to the Lord, she is the most exuberant Christian.

Wen Chuan Wang of Vancouver, B.C., wrote of the film showing in his area:

> It was a spectacular sight: the hall was fully packed with people, cars filled all the parking spaces of the nearby streets, and people were still coming! Never had we seen anything like this before. What was happening? The "Queen" was coming! The first color gospel film in Chinese was to be presented that night by the Chinese Christian Mission. Most of the Chinese Christians were present, and many had brought along several nonbelieving friends. There was quite a number of Canadian friends too, being attracted by the posters all over town. The seats were occupied in no time.
>
> What really amazed us was the response to the showing of the film in the coffee shop in the basement of the Salvation Army. The audience was a group of hippies. It turned a smoky dirty den suddenly into a quiet and respectable meeting place.

There are many incidents of how the Lord used the "Queen" movie to draw people to Himself. In San Francisco, the Chinese newspapers publicized the movie. The Chinese owner of a big business in Chinatown saw the advertisement. He rushed to see it. When he got there, he could hardly find a place to stand. This was the fifth time that the movie had been shown that day. Later Mr. T. wrote to me:

"I never heard of you nor read your book. But when I was looking at the movie, I could not restrain my tears. Finally I stood up to accept the Lord. When I looked around, I saw over one hundred standing to express their acceptance of our Saviour Jesus Christ."

Mr. T. borrowed a copy of my book from a friend and read it to his family. The members of his family also accepted the

Lord. Somehow he found my address. He said that he did not know where to buy the book, so he was copying it!

Miss W., the president of a seminary in Singapore, wrote,

> "I remembered that when you spoke in Ku-lang-su, a beautiful island across from Amoy, China, about 1918, I heard you, and many others believed because of your witness. When I was in America in 1968 I wanted to see you so I could report to friends in Singapore, but I could not make it. Praise the Lord, your movie came here and was shown to different groups who were inspired by it. Then it came right to our seminary! The whole school was greatly moved. We did not know how to express our appreciation, so we are sending you a little love gift. We will continue to pray for you, asking our Heavenly Father to use you."

A Chinese university student came to have an interview with me in preparation for showing the movie in various university centers on the East Coast. He asked me, "How does it make you feel to have your biography made into a movie?"

"It makes me feel humble," I answered. "I pray that the Lord may help me so to live that I may not disgrace Him, nor disappoint my friends."

I shared with him a little story about humility. For years the Lord has been teaching me about the biblical principle of dying to self. It is wonderful when one puts himself on the cross and Christ on the throne. A dead man has no feelings and cares not what others say, for he is dead. How I long that I may learn to exalt Jesus in every way and to lead every one who enters my darkened room to meet the Lord Himself.

Years ago in Kuling, a beautiful summer mountain resort in China, there was a spring of clear water in the garden of our home. Because it was some distance from our kitchen, we brought some hollowed-out bamboo poles and fitted them end to end to pipe the water to our kitchen door. One day when we were expecting guests for dinner, the cook suddenly rushed in to say that there was no water coming from the pipe. I hurried up the side of the hill to the spring to find out the reason. The cool, fresh water was still bubbling up from the ground, and the bamboo poles were still carefully fitted together, lying on the green grass. I started to pull the poles apart, and there I found a large, fat green frog firmly wedged inside one of the poles. It completely blocked the way so that no water could get through.

When I saw that proud, fat frog, my heart immediately bowed at my Lord's feet and I cried, "My Rock, my Saviour, search me and see if there be any hidden sin, any swelling pride blocking the pipeline of my heart and stopping the overflow of Your Spirit." Later, remembering this incident, I composed the following lines that may be sung to the tune "Nettleton," commonly used with "Come, Thou Fount of Every Blessing."

> Saviour, make me always humble,
> Not for honor, not for fame,
> Saviour, fill me, empty vessel,
> Full of praises to Thy name.
> Never let me hide Thy glory,
> Idle words Thy truth conceal,
> Save me from all pride; before Thee,
> Worthy Lamb, I humbly kneel.

Mrs. Torrey Shih, a well-known Chinese writer, carried *Queen of the Dark Chamber* day and night for three months. Then she wrote a Chinese play of it. It was first dramatized in Manila, Philippines in 1964, then in the United States and Canada. The following is a brief report from Manila:

You must be very anxious to hear about the presentation of our drama last January 3. Well, here it is!

There was a big crowd of more than five hundred people, each dressed in his or her best, in that large air-conditioned auditorium, waiting to witness one of the greatest dramas ever presented in local church history, if not the local Chinese dramatic life. The curtain opened promptly at 8:00, the atmosphere was very good, the actors and actresses were ready after four solid months of training and prayer, the lighting was the best in the country—and on top of all this, the free and liberal working of the Holy Spirit made the 2½ hour presentation a success. Praise and glory to Him who both began and accomplished it. Your prayers as well as those of people all over the world did not go in vain.

Do you know that over DZAS, the most powerful station in the South East Asia, otherwise known as the Far East Broadcasting Company, your biography has been narrated in a weekly fifteen-minute program? It started January 1, and will probably be through in three or four months. The narrator, Mr. Teddy Young, is an active youth leader of our church. Do pray that this may become a blessing to many listeners."

Several years ago the Lord called a lady to join The Evangelical Alliance Mission radio station in Taiwan. It gave her a wonderful opportunity to dedicate her pen to the Lord to write for gospel broadcasts every day. She had always had a secret longing to work on my book for broadcasting. It had to be carefully rewritten to adapt the story for radio listeners so they could visualize the living witness. She reports,

There were many difficulties. At the beginning of this year, God gave me the courage to see it through. While I was writing, I flowed tears again many times for the witness of your life. This summer my co-workers and I were overjoyed to have the unexpected surprise of actually corresponding with you.

We never dreamed it was possible to receive a handwritten letter from you! We now feel like partakers with you in your glorious spiritual fight and are one heart with you. All in all, we unite in praise to the Lord that we have been given a little part by the Lord in such a great opportunity to introduce this chosen vessel, you, as a handmaid for the Lord, to inspire brothers and sisters behind the bamboo curtain in China!

The TEAM radio station broadcast to mainland China the drama form of *Queen of the Dark Chamber* in eighty-six broadcasts of fifteen minutes each, commencing in June 1973.

TWENTY-TWO

More Dramas Unfold

One Sunday morning a Chinese friend stayed with us while Susanna went to church. Suddenly the quiet was shattered by a fierce ringing of the back doorbell. Our friend said, "There is a tall American with a terrible face demanding to come in to see you. He has come all the way from Maine. I'm afraid to let him in!"

I said, "Let us just trust the Lord. Let him in."

When he strode into my chamber, I thought our hour to meet the Lord had come. "I have read your book, so I came to see you. I am going to kill my wife and my six children and myself!" he ranted.

As a helpless invalid in bed, unable to defend myself, I was sure he was going to kill us, too. I put our defense in the hands of the Lord and cried out to Him in my heart for wisdom for what to tell this man. I softly answered, "If I talked to you for three days it wouldn't answer your questions. Let us each take a Bible. Ask the Lord to speak to you." For three or four hours God guided my dizzy head to point him to one Scripture after another to show him his condition and the way out through Christ, not through murder and suicide.

Finally I sensed a breakthrough as he asked me pointedly, "Why are you smiling all the time? What are you so happy about being old and sick so long and lying in bed?"

"It is Jesus who lives in my heart. He gives me joy." I told

him that when I opened my heart to Christ even the leaves
and grass and flowers all seemed to change color. The whole
world was transformed. "Your life is black and terrible to you
because you don't have Jesus in your heart."

His intense face finally broke into a smile. He rose and
declared, "Miss Tsai, I want Jesus to come into my heart. I
will follow His teaching. I promise I won't kill myself and my
family. I will trust in God and go to church!"

After we prayed, he held my hand and with tears said,
"May I give you a kiss?"

Since I was almost eighty years old and unable to answer
no under such circumstances, I accepted it as a "holy kiss."
As he left my stage and marched out the door, I could only
lie there exhausted and praise God, not only for preserving
our lives to serve Him a little longer, but also for the privilege
of pointing another soul, who had been going in the direction of darkness, to turn to His light.

Another time, prison doors swung open for two cars full
of women prisoners with their guards to drive four hours
from Muncy, Pennsylvania, to visit me. One of the guards
told us that it was the first time such a group was allowed to
visit in a private home. After I spoke to them, the prisoners
crowded around me in parting, saying that they wanted
Jesus to live in their hearts forever.

Standing at the back of the room while I talked to the
prisoners were five Chinese, most of whom had been born
in Tanzania, Africa. They had come to Paradise as the result
of a visit to Africa by Reverend Moses Chow, executive director of Ambassadors for Christ, Inc. Right after the prisoners walked out, they came to my bedside and said, "All five
of us want to accept Jesus as our Saviour." Not long afterward they were baptized, and since then they have been
faithful in attending church.

Three days before Easter 1958, the American Bible Society called from New York and told us the following cable had been received from Hong Kong: "Chinese Phonetic account urgently requires remittance US dollars six thousand (6,000)." At last the phonetic Bible would be off the press!

I wish you could have been here with us when we were going to sign the check. I asked China Mary to sign, and she asked me to sign it. We were scared, because it was the biggest check we had ever signed in our lives. After we prayed at least a dozen times, asking God to bless everyone who had helped in preparing the Bible, we both signed the check.

On the night of a great snowstorm one year, cars were stalled all along Lincoln Highway in front of our house. Unfortunate travelers were suffering from exposure, so we opened our doors, inviting them in. Soon our house was full. Because of electric failure, we had no light, no heat, and no water. Among the travelers was an elderly grandmother, as well as a baby with pneumonia, who was crying all night outside my room.

Susanna gathered up all the supplies she could find and cooked a whole pot of food for the snowbound travelers. Just as the truck drivers were ready to lie down to sleep on the floor in our big parlor, a phone call came saying that Pequea Valley High School was kindly opening its doors and wanted the truck drivers to go there. The snowstorm actually lasted a whole week.

One young man, a "rock and roller," danced around to amuse the guests. At last he came into my room and pleaded, "Let me show you some rock and roll."

Was my room really going to become his stage? "All right," I answered, "but I want to make a bargain with you.

Among the travelers was an elderly grandmother and a baby.

You can rock and roll for me if you will promise to go out and read my book afterward."

"It's a deal!" he cried. He really rocked and rolled more than half an hour. I was his only audience! Then he settled down and started to read my book. The next morning his manner had changed completely. "I want to accept Jesus," he said. Later he came back as a sincere Christian to visit me from Pittsburgh.

"Oh, Miss Tsai, do you remember my mother, Mayhill?" one visitor eagerly began. "She was one of the seven normal school pupils in China who were expelled by the dean, Miss Plum, for going to your home to study the Bible. You wrote in your book how she and over seventy pupils believed in the Lord. Well, now my wife and I and two daughters also love the Lord. Do you know that Miss Plum, who turned to the Lord and served Him so fervently, was kept in a Communist prison for eighteen years and died there? She witnessed that she would rather die than compromise her faith in the Lord. What a brave soldier of the cross! We want to follow her example!"

How my heart was lifted. My praise overflowed to the Lord as I remembered. It had been a difficult decision I had made so many years ago in China that made possible the story of salvation which this Chinese brother in Christ and his family were bringing me.

China Mary had double pneumonia a little over a year before she went to be with the Lord. She was almost unconscious one day as I was taking care of her, when a woman asked to see her. The woman came in and told the following story which had been unknown to me. "My husband was an alcoholic. China Mary quietly helped us. She also helped my husband enter Keswick Colony for alcoholics to break his awful appetite. Praise the Lord! He is now free from it and has become a very earnest Christian. Here is sixty dollars for China Mary. I owe her a very great deal! I will remember her all my life with unspeakable gratitude. We will try to live like her!"

Later a Mr. B. suddenly appeared at our back door. He was very anxious to see China Mary, so we requested that because of her weakness, he stay only five minutes. He held her hand and choked with emotion. Tears came to his eyes as he spoke gently, telling her that she had helped him so much spiritually. He also told her that he owed her a great deal of money and that because of her real Christian love, all of his children were following the Lord. He gave her one hundred dollars as he left, promising that by the Lord's power he would try to follow China Mary's example and help others. Both he and his oldest son are now pastors!

A pastor from another state had asked me repeatedly if I would see the parents of his church secretary. They had rejected her. Three times I had to refuse to see them because of prior engagements, but this time they came anyway.

It was very difficult to talk with the couple, because the father monopolized the conversation. He seemed to know everything, just like an encyclopedia. As is my custom with talkative people, I let him talk on, praying silently until he was all talked out. Finally he became quiet. Then he asked me abruptly, "If people believe in Jesus secretly in their hearts, isn't that enough? Why is it necessary to make it known publicly?"

I prayed and answered him simply, "It is like marriage. When you want to get married, why should you have a ceremony and guests and a public occasion? Will that increase the love between two people?"

"No," he answered.

"In a wedding ceremony you are announcing to your relatives and friends that you and your wife have become one person," I continued. "Conversion or being born again truly takes place in your heart, privately. Please read Matthew 10:32-33."

He read it aloud very distinctly: "Whosoever therefore shall confess me before men, him will I confess also before my Father which is in heaven. But whosoever shall deny me before men, him will I also deny before my Father which is in heaven."

"Confessing Christ by being baptized and joining a local church is letting people know you are united with Christ, that you are on His side," I stressed.

Later the pastor came back for this couple. To my surprise, the father stood up and asked the pastor, "When is your church going to have a baptismal service again?"

"In November," the pastor answered.

"Then put down the names of my wife and myself," the father said. "We want to publicly confess Jesus Christ as our Lord and Saviour."

I was told later that the father was truly born again. Nothing could keep him from telling others about salvation in Jesus Christ.

A certain group had come from New Jersey so I could speak to them. When I finished, most of them went into another room to buy books. I noticed a man who had been sitting in the back of my room, silently listening to every word I spoke. While the leader of the group was talking to me about some church business, this man suddenly came to my bedside, demanding, "Who taught you Buddhism?"

I answered him promptly, "Yang Ren-san." He surprised me by bowing low to me.

"It is unbelievable that anyone indoctrinated by Yang would become a Christian!" He shook his head.

It was true. Yang Ren-san was a former Chinese ambassador to France and well educated in many fields. An ardent and well-trained Buddhist, he turned his mansion into a center to teach Buddhism. He had a print shop in his home where he published Buddhist materials, and he built a temple in his back yard, where devotees lived. I remember staying there many nights with my friends, eating only vegetarian foods. Three of us girls especially used to pray day and night. It was our custom to go to Ambassador Yang's home every Sunday afternoon to learn about Buddhism. We were well brainwashed.

This gentleman confessed, "I actually came here today as a spy. I was far from Christianity. I wanted to catch you in some error or expose you by proving that you did not know what you were talking about. I could not catch you. When I came I was far, far away from following Jesus. Now maybe I am one inch away."

I replied, "One inch or one mile, it doesn't matter how far away you are, if you aren't *in*!" Then I witnessed further about my Lord to him. Later, my co-worker Grace took him into another room and led him to an open acceptance of the Lord.

TWENTY-THREE

The Chase to Philadelphia

My hand shook as I reached for the phone in the pre-dawn of a cold November morning and dialed the number of our friend Leona Choy in Silver Spring, Maryland. I breathed a prayer. The telephone continued to ring. If our friend were not available, we would surely not be able to make the long trip to the hospital by ambulance.

A sleepy "Hello," then an enthusiastic and willing agreement, hasty arrangements, and our friend was on her way to us. She drove the 125-mile trip in record time.

The anticipated worst had happened. For two days, China Mary had had excruciating eye pain and a headache which she had tried, in her accustomed manner, to hide from us all. When her suffering and pain became no longer bearable, we found out and called the doctor. He had warned us several years before that if China Mary developed acute pain in her eye, the glaucoma would be out of hand and any delay might prove fatal. In less than four hours we made all the arrangements on our side and were on our way.

I say "we" advisedly, because Leona's station wagon, one of the largest models, was loaded to capacity with not only China Mary, the patient, but our co-worker Susanna *and* myself. Leona had scant visibility through the rear window because of the "essentials" we had to take with us. In China, literally everything that one would need had to be taken along to the hospital. Families would even bring in food for the patient's meals and care for him. We had no experience with hospitals in America, so we wanted to be prepared. Our Chinese eye specialist, Dr. Huang, on the staff of Wills Eye Hospital in Philadelphia, knew us well. He did not try to dissuade me when I insisted I was coming along to the hospital with China Mary. We had not been separated for a single day or night in the twenty-three years since returning to America. There was just no way I would let her—aged, nearly blind, and in pain—out of my sight to go to the hospital by herself!

Dr. Huang miraculously (it was he who used the word!) succeeded in having me admitted simultaneously as a patient with China Mary, though the hospital was already overcrowded. The records showed that I was to have extensive tests with specialized optical equipment, which he had felt for a long time was necessary. The second miracle was to get permission from the hospital administration to allow Susanna to stay in the same room with us as a "nurse's aid." We agreed to pay the patient's rate for her as well. To obtain an empty room for *three* was the final miracle, but our Lord is used to doing the impossible.

The doctor had instructed that eye drops be put into China Mary's eyes every fifteen minutes to ease the pressure and pain. This had to be continued even during the journey to the hospital. As for me, I had left the Leaman home for such a long ride only once in those twenty-three years, and that was to appear for my American permanent residence exam in Philadelphia. I could not even sit or be pushed in a wheelchair, because motion sickness would immediately set in. To contemplate riding in a car as far as Philadelphia again was like a trip to the moon without the benefit of a pressurized capsule to offset my nausea.

I implored Leona, "Drive ever so slowly. Stop by the side of the road every fifteen minutes so I can recover my balance."

I did not fully grasp her tactful attempt to explain about "regulations on the expressway" and something about "minimum speed." I only knew that I might die before we got there! Dutifully, she kept the speed to a rapid crawl and regularly signaled to pull aside on the four-lane highway to allow me to rest and have Susanna put the eye drops in China Mary's eyes. All of us were perspiring with tension as the trip progressed. We prayed continually, sometimes aloud, sometimes under our breath, that the Lord would see us through.

When Leona reached the final junction spilling the Pennsylvania Turnpike traffic into the Schuylkill Expressway to inner city Philadelphia, she parked in an area marked "Emergency stopping only." We applied the eye drops again, and I clung to the seat in front of me to keep the world from swimming by as the heavy trucks and madly rushing cars zoomed close to our windows. To shield both of us from the intense light, we had put cardboard on the side windows. The light snow that had fallen a few days previously reflected an unbearable glare. Leona had not shared with us her lack of familiarity with how to get to the hospital once within the inner city. Indeed, she didn't have time to consult a map or ask for directions, for we called her out of bed and from her home and family at 5 A.M. She had committed it to the Lord, trusting that when the time came, God would provide.

Before she got the car in gear again, the sound of a siren shrilled in our ears and two police cars screeched alongside. A burly policeman in natty uniform and dark glasses strode up pompously to Leona's window. "And just what do you think you are doing? You are parked in an emergency zone!"

"Officer," Leona replied, "this *is* an emergency. I am taking these elderly friends to the hospital as fast as I can get them there."

Immediately sizing up the situation with sympathetic understanding, after Leona had confided to him that she wasn't sure of the way, he motioned his fellow officer to proceed to other calls, and beckoned, saying, "Just follow me. Ignore the stoplights and the speed limit as long as you stay right behind me. I'll guide you to the hospital."

We took off—literally, I thought! At least I felt as if I were in an airplane, for he had not given Leona a chance to explain that we had to drive at a snail's pace for the sake of my nausea. For the first time in my life I saw the flashing, rotating red light in action on top of a police car. For the last half hour of our trip, the officer sped us straight through the morning rush-hour traffic, zooming through red lights and weaving in and out of lanes of cars. I believe I must have fallen into a daze or faint. I expected that my next waking vision would be that of my heavenly Father at the gate of heaven!

We screamed to a halt, right at the admitting door of the hospital. After he found our Chinese Dr. Huang, the officer tipped his hat to acknowledge our gratitude, and disappeared. The policeman had been our angel sent by the Lord! For God has promised, "For he shall give his angels charge over thee, to keep thee in all thy ways . . . lest thou dash thy foot against a stone" (Psalm 91:11-12). Or, in our case, "lest we get lost in the maze of downtown Philadelphia!"

The entrance elevator was only a few yards from the admitting door, and Leona ordered two wheelchairs. Interns

helped us out of the car to the elevator. Leona had to re-
main with the car, temporarily double-parked at the entrance, with our baggage. At the same time she requested
that the elevator operator return for our "essentials." As
instructed, the old man returned to the main floor entrance,
anticipating a little overnight bag for each of the three
"grandmas", as he called us. When Leona began pulling out
armload after armload of paraphernalia, equipment, and
"strange things tied up in bundles like from the old country,"
he could hardly believe his eyes.

"You're putting me on!" he said, aghast. Besides innum-
erable suitcases and boxes, there were armrests, a walker,
teapot, herb tea, thermos bottles, foodstuffs, pillows, blankets, and other things. "No one, but *no one* has ever come
into the hospital with all this gear! They won't allow it upstairs, and then I'll have to take it all the way down again.
Come on, lady, give it up!" he pleaded.

After Leona had finally convinced him that each bulky
item was critical to the survival of the three "grandmas" and
a substantial tip had been given to deaden the pain, Leona
began her ascent by elevator to the floor where we had been
assigned a room. Still shaking his head and clicking his
tongue, the elevator operator deposited everything in the
hall, which was now full of nurses, interns, and orderlies, who
had been alerted that there was an invasion of some sort.
Somewhere along the line it was noised abroad in the hospital that there was a Chinese queen and her attendants moving into a private suite!

But everything was far from under regal control in the
hospital room to which we had been ushered. The room was
big, in a corner by the elevator, and was set up with two
regulation single hospital beds, and one low camp cot by the
wall prepared for the "nurse's aide" who was to be in the

room with us. I was wheeled in after China Mary had already been lifted to one of the single beds. I motioned for
the nurse to push me over to the camp cot. "That's the one I
want to sleep on," I declared.

"But that's for your helper," argued the young nurse.
"That is not for a patient. I can't put you there!"

"I *must* stay there," I said. "I can never lie on a high bed. I
have a balance problem. I would be dizzy and fall off!"

"There are bars at the side of the bed," she pleaded
nervously.

"I don't want bars. I want to sleep on the low cot!"

"Sorry, lady, I can't let you!"

"Oh, but you *must!*" I insisted.

"I have to call the supervisor!" she said weakly, parking
me near the bed and running off.

In a moment, a buxom, commanding lady in white appeared with a clipboard and papers, which she checked over
swiftly, peering over her bifocals. She turned to Susanna.
"And just which ones are the patients?" she demanded.

"They are," Susanna said, pointing to China Mary and
me. "I am their companion. I've come along to help."

"Patients can *only* stay in regulation hospital beds. Any
violation will be cause for insurance coverage cancellation,
and then all of us will be in for a big heap of trouble!" she
thundered.

By that time Dr. Huang had appeared on the scene and
surveyed the mounting drama. He tenderly but firmly explained to me that I had to stay in the hospital bed. I agreed
finally, asking the Lord to preserve me on that white mountain as He had in many valleys before. The head nurse was
so pleased to avoid a further scene that she kissed me and
thanked me for complying.

The examinations started almost immediately for both of

us. We were wheeled downstairs where, in room after room, eye-testing machines stared menacingly at us. They were indeed a testing and a torture for both of us. For China Mary was suffering from her weakness and pain, and I from my motion sickness, fatigue, and disruption of any semblance of my usual schedule. That night we were not returned to our room until 10:30—we who always prepared for bed at 6 P.M.

The next day China Mary and I went through even more detailed examinations. They continued all day, until at 11 P.M. the head surgeon pulled my wheelchair aside and said, "I am sorry to tell you that Miss Leaman had a stroke once in her eye which left scar tissue; this prevents us from operating on her after all."

"What would happen if she were operated on?" I asked fearfully.

"She might have a massive hemorrhage and die on the operating table," the doctor answered soberly.

"What will happen if she does not have the operation?" I ventured.

"She will die in terrible pain and suffering," the doctor answered reluctantly.

As the astronauts enroute to the moon kept constant contact with their Houston, Texas, headquarters for directions and corrections, so I kept my heart turned by prayer to my headquarters, the Lord Jesus. I asked Him now to give me His clear direction. He did. I concluded, "Well, if she has to face death one way or the other, I would rather have her go to the Lord on the operating table than to die in lingering pain and suffering."

"Very well," the chief surgeon said. "Let me call some of the other doctors for a consultation." It was 11:30 P.M.

Three American doctors joined her for a whispered discussion.

After what seemed like a long time, I was again called, as if to a courtroom. "Are you willing to sign the paper of responsibility in case of a hemorrhage on the operating table?"

My Lord clearly guided me to say, "Yes, I am ready to sign."

It was almost one o'clock in the morning by the time we were wheeled back to our room. During the night various nurses came in to prepare China Mary for surgery. I truly felt my merciful Lord Jesus' constant companionship.

Early next morning, Leona returned from her place of lodging. At once we prayed together, asking our Lord to be the Great Physician. Soon the attendants came to transfer China Mary to the operating room. I was amazed how smoothly they moved her to the rolling table from her bed. It was so skillfully, quickly, and quietly done. During my long illness, I had entered seven different hospitals in China and St. Barbar's Hospital in Osaka, Japan. But I had not seen such tender handling before. Leona followed the rolling bed but had to stop about ten feet away from the final swinging door, on the other side of which patients were waiting their turns for surgery.

Again my heart checked in with my heavenly headquarters. "Everything under control." Yes, all was under my Lord's control!

China Mary was operated on. After four hours, Dr. Huang, still in his surgical gown, rushed breathlessly to our room: "Praise the Lord!" he said. "The operation is a success!" Skillful doctors had performed the needed repair which the Great Physician had taken care of. China Mary would have to be most careful, and the emergency could recur, but we thanked the Lord again for His providence that we were able to get there on time. My examinations gave the doctors a much better diagnosis of my eye problems and enabled them to preserve what sight I do have.

We had requested not to have visitors, as we needed our full rest. Nevertheless, we were besieged with calls and inquiries from kind friends. One dear old friend did get past the hospital vigilance to our bedside, anyway. It was Dr. William Miller, officially retired after being a missionary for forty years, but far from stopping his work for the Lord. He was responsible for preparing the Iranian translation of *Queen of the Dark Chamber.* I was told that each time he rode on the hospital elevator he witnessed to the people around him and gave them tracts. Once a missionary, always a missionary!

We stayed in the hospital for ten days. As I was about to leave, I gave a copy of my book to the surgeon and one to the head nurse. Somehow the news got around, and before we left the hospital, thirty-five resident doctors and nurses requested copies. I could not count how many came asking me to autograph their books.

The trip home to Leaman Place was less eventful and more joyous. The Lord had seen us through another lesson in His classroom, entitled "Trust Me, even to Philadelphia!"

TWENTY-FOUR

My Godmother's Hands

When my godmother and I were in fairly good health, we often speculated about our future. I always insisted, "If the Lord should tarry and we have to be separated, I want you to pray that God will allow me to go to heaven first. I would never survive without you! You are the one with such strong faith in the Lord. I am weak."

China Mary would always gently reprove me, "You must not say that, dear. You have to let the Lord decide whatever He sees best."

When she was taken ill for the last time, I realized it was serious. I not only prayed myself, but repeated to her, "Godmother, please pray that God may take me first, because you can face troubles and I can't." I also told her, "If the Lord should take you first, I want you to know that I will refuse to see people; I will not write; I will not do anything. I will just sit and wait! I will 'close my store,' as we Chinese say."

Sick as she was, she whispered patiently, "Christiana, take it back. Take it back! You must follow His will."

On the night of January 19, 1972, my heart was pounding with apprehension. I sensed that she was slipping fast. I insisted, against literally everyone's orders, that she lie in my bed with me. We could not be separated at such a precious time. During her whole illness she lay beside me on my bed, often semiconsciously tossing and turning so that I was al-

175

most pushed off the bed. Day and night, week after week, she had become increasingly ill. On this night the kind nurse held one hand and I held the other.

Her hand had been our only means of communication for some time. She could not see anymore and could only mumble a few words, but her hand reached over constantly to touch me. It was my godmother's hands that had lovingly and patiently cared for me for forty-one long years while I was bedridden. For those first sixteen years that the doctors had not been able to diagnose my illness, when I was sick with fever, all my knuckles had cracked open and eight fingernails disappeared. My godmother had soaked my hands in lukewarm water and gently rubbed my fingers day after day. In order to force-feed me and save my life when I could not swallow, she had fed me orange juice a drop at a time, gently stroking it down my throat for a whole month. Even to the day when she was suddenly taken sick, her warm hand reached to my icy-cold hands as my persistent malaria chills came on every day. She would take my cold hands in her soft warm hands, saying, "Let me *wu-wu* them" (*wu-wu* means "to warm up" in Chinese). Above all, those dear hands had prepared the whole phonetic Bible for my illiterate countrymen in China so they could read and understand the Word of God. And when we came to the United States, her hands had prepared many meals and ministered to the Chinese officers, seamen, and students. It would take pages more to tell what those dear hands did for me and others all those years.

As I held her hand on that final night, the nurse repeatedly tried to listen to her faint heartbeat. Suddenly China Mary became very quiet. She raised her shoulders just a little. I whispered hoarsely, "Godmother, Godmother!"

She answered, "Um."

I called to her again. Everything became quiet. No answer.

The nurse said, "She has gone from us. I am sending for the doctor."

What a thunderbolt! When her hand finally stopped reaching toward me, I knew she was in the presence of the Lord, as Paul said, "absent from the body, . . . present with the Lord" (2 Corinthians 5:8).

Dr. Robert Snader arrived. After his examination, he said sternly to me, "Christiana, I insist that you leave this room. She has gone. You must take care of yourself now. You have to get some rest!" This doctor was very kind and thoughtful of me. He had taken care of both of us for more than twenty years. I told him that I wanted to stay with her a while, even though her spirit was in heaven. He answered very strictly, "No such thing! Go out and rest!"

While he was writing the death certificate in our sitting room, the thoughtful funeral director, Mr. Brown, who had heard the doctor's remark, privately whispered to me, "Christiana, I understand. Never mind. It will take me two hours to make preparations to come back for her." His place was nearby, almost within sight of our home, so I knew it actually might have taken him only ten minutes to return. But he knew my aching heart and that I needed to spend more time with her. He was a church elder and had been our good friend for many years. When we worked with the officers, seamen, and students, he brought his folding chairs and set them up for the large meetings. He always said, "I want to share in what the Lord is doing."

It was late at night. Everyone was out of my room except my godmother and me, and she was now beholding her dear Saviour's face. I held her cold hand. We had worked together for the Lord fifty-eight years for His glory, separated only for the two years she was in the concentration camp after Pearl Harbor. Now she had entered heaven's gates. This parting scene brought back memories of when she entered the concentration camp in China. About fifty of our Chinese Christian friends came on bicycles to accompany her to the camp as she rode in a rickshaw. I could not go along because I was not well enough, so I stayed back with my lonely tears, just watching her umbrella disappear in the distance. The Japanese guards stood at the gate. She got off the rickshaw, picked up her bundle, and passed through the gate all alone. All her friends watched tearfully as her shadow disappeared.

In all my eighty-two years, this was the first time I had ever seen the fearful power of death tearing away a loved one. I longed to take her place and die for her, but death paid no attention to me. As I looked at her hands, finally still, I praised the Lord Jesus Christ for His wonderful salvation. I knew my godmother was with Him forever. I thanked Him for the assurance that by His saving grace I would meet her in our heavenly home. I also understood now the utter terror of anyone facing death without believing in Jesus and of passing all alone into the great unknown.

Because of the hope of our resurrection and the assurance of eternal life through Jesus Christ, my separation from my godmother, although sorrowful for the time being, had in it the joyous seeds of victory and hope that we would be together again someday in His presence. So at this time I had no tears. I could not even pray.

Suddenly I seemed to see a vision of a vast wilderness, with dark clouds overhead. A figure appeared, walking very fast toward a bottomless pit. I was not able to distinguish the features. Then I seemed to hear a voice calling three times, "Christiana, stop that person!"

I suddenly woke from my vision and realized the Lord was patiently teaching me a lesson. There was still work for me to do for the Lord. I bowed my head and prayed, "Lord, forgive me for what I said. I do not want to hurt Thy feelings with my self-pity nor turn against my dear godmother's wishes. Lord, help me follow Thy leading, whatsoever Thou wouldst have me do."

Old folks really don't want new clothes. I was already eighty-two. Could I really expect a "new garment"? Did I dare pray that my godmother's Christlike life and winsome spiritual witness, like "Eiljah's mantle," might fall upon me, so that my hands also might in every way serve the risen and coming again Lord Jesus Christ?

Then the reality of the practical details of China Mary's funeral dawned upon me. In China I had never participated directly in any funerals. When my father had died, my brothers had taken charge of everything. I had been away when my mother died. What did I know of all the responsibilities for burial arrangements, estates, and legal matters in America? Here I was in a foreign country, unfamiliar with its traditions and customs. I could scarcely believe that the Lord put into my hands the management of all three of the funerals of those dearest to me: the Leaman sisters and Cousin Mary W. In the midst of my personal grief, I had to handle the estates, deal with lawyers and courts, act as executrix, and attend to legal matters! China Mary, previously capable and practical-minded to handle any emergency throughout my long illness, had been too physically weak to manage the home-going arrangements of both Cousin Mary and Sister Lucy, who had died eight and four years before, respectively. And, now, upon her departure, I was left alone without her wise counsel and patience to direct me. But the Lord was my "very present help in trouble" (Psalm 46:1) as always.

After the funeral, all my kind friends and helpers were tired. Suddenly the back doorbell rang. Our faithful co-worker Susanna opened it to confront a well-dressed American man. "Who are you?" she inquired.

He answered abruptly, "I'm not going to tell you my name." He walked through the dining room, where Miss Ng requested him to sign the guest book. Again he refused, saying, "I'm not going to sign my name."

When he walked into my room I could tell with my dim eyes that he was handsome and young. The first thing I asked was his name. Refusing again to answer, he sat down right on the corner of the couch where my godmother used to sit early each morning. He covered his face with his hands and began to cry loudly. In all my life I had never seen a young man cry that hard. I thought that he must have known my godmother and he was crying with grief at her home-going. I tried asking him different questions, but there was no response. I prayed, "Lord, I don't know the heart-aches of this gentleman. You know them. Speak to him and comfort him."

Meanwhile, my co-workers were suspicious that he was a bad man who had come to harm me. They sat outside my room, carefully watching him. Finally I said to him, by the help of the Holy Spirit, "Sir, we are all made to die once and after that the judgement" (see Hebrews 9:27). He paid no attention but kept on crying. The Spirit helped me to go on and explain to him what salvation is and what eternal life means to believers.

It was growing late and Miss Ng came in to say, "Sir, don't you want to come to the parlor and rest awhile?"

By that time he had stopped crying so loudly, but he was still quietly sobbing. He stood up, fixed his eyes on me for about a minute, then said, "Thank you. You have given me the key to salvation. Good-bye!" To this day I don't know who he was, nor have I ever seen him again. God knows.

As soon as he left, a friend came in and said, "What shall we do? I know how exhausted you are, but a group of American young people has come. They didn't even know that China Mary has gone to be with the Lord."

I answered, "We must let them come in." I remembered China Mary's constant attitude of "restful availability" for whatever the Lord brought into our lives. "I will just say hello to them."

Those precious young people quietly marched into my room. My eyes were so tired and dim I could hardly see them. I said to them, "Precious in the sight of the LORD is the death of his saints" (Psalm 116:15). Then I shared with them for about ten minutes how wonderful salvation is.

Later my friend asked me, "Did you see the hands of six young people raised to accept Christ when you invited them to believe?"

How patient and forgiving the Lord Jesus is! "He restoreth my soul" (Psalm 23:3). Although He had just led me through the valley of the shadow of death, His rod and staff not only were comforting me, but they were also lovingly forcing me to keep on comforting and ministering to others. He did not allow me to "close my store." "I must be about my Father's business" as usual!

Long-distance calls, telegrams, and letters of sympathy poured in from friends who were wondering what I was going to do without China Mary or any relatives in this country. Indeed, as my godmother, she had been more than a mother to me. Three years before, when we had put up a

cemetery marker for China Mary's sister, Lucy, we had decided to put all three of our names on it. China Mary wanted
the following words inscribed on the stone: "Jesus will never
leave us" (see Hebrews 13:5). Yes, my godmother had to
leave me, but Jesus will never leave me.

I asked my friends to kindly remember me in their prayers
so that (1) I would not be anxious about the next step. My
godmother used to remind me every morning, "As thou
goest, step by step, I will open the way before thee" (Prov-
erbs 4:12, Hebrew translation); (2) I would not anticipate the
future. It is in the Lord's hand alone; (3) I would not choose
my way, for His way is higher; and (4) I would not carry the
heavy load of imaginary thoughts on my own back. He
careth for me! I knew my Lord wanted me to go forward.

TWENTY-FIVE

Longing for Home

Life is like a train. There are many stops. One gets off here, another there, along the way. So many of my friends have gotten off already when the train arrived at their stations. When I came to this country in 1949, China Mary, her sister Lucy, Cousin Mary, a maid, a couple who came here to help us, and the family doctor were all aboard the first day. Now all seven have gone to be with the Lord. I, the weakest one, am still here. I do not ask why. I am among the few of my generation still left on the train. My ticket is in my heavenly Conductor's hand—He will let me know when I arrive at my stop. Meanwhile, the Lord must have a purpose for me to live so long.

In 1949, we had begun as a most joyful and harmonious quartet in Paradise, Pennsylvania: Cousin Mary W., Sister Lucy, Godmother China Mary, and me. We always served the Lord with one heart and one mind. Mary W.'s one wish was so often expressed: "all together." Whenever I held a meeting in my darkened room, the three prayer warriors never failed to quietly pray for me in the sitting room—we four were one.

In 1964, our dear "all together" Mary W. was the first of our quartet to enter glory. By the mercy of the Lord, the trio continued.

In 1968, Sister Lucy was summoned to be with the Lord.

183

I often marvel at God's mercy and goodness. He continued to lead China Mary and me to play a duet. I must confess my weakness and say that I often "hanged my harp upon the willow" (see Psalm 137:2) and "sat down under a juniper tree" (1 Kings 19:4). But my godmother's devotion to the Lord never wavered and always kept me steady. Her prayer life was more important than her food. Only the Lord knows how she helped and encouraged me to go forward!

On January 19, 1972, exactly twenty-three years to the day since she and I had left China's shore, she was called to her "new job" in her heavenly home. Every four years one of us had dropped out of the quartet. We know there are no reruns of the film of life. So here I am alone! I can only bow my head and say that I know my master Architect has guided my steps "by the skilfulness of his hands" (Psalm 78:72). By His grace, I take up my harp and go on playing a solo.

The day dawned like any other day. Though it was mid-winter, the sun rose brilliantly, though late, and reflected against the new fallen snow. I could see its rays seeking entrance to my room through the cracks in the dark curtains around my windows. But I dared not look at it, blinking my sensitive eyes away from its glow.

That morning my eyes also blinked away a great flood of tears. I was trying to hold them back by a dam of self-control, though some trickles still made their way through my eyelids and splashed against my pillow. Today was the anniversary of the home-going of my dear godmother.

After she joined the Lord, I did not believe that I could survive if left alone. I did not want to go on. I begged the Lord to take me, too, right away, so that we would not be separated. How wonderful it would be to behold the glory of the face of the Lord side by side with my companion of a lifetime! How we would together enjoy finding out the mysterious things now revealed in His presence! She would be able to see and I would be able to walk! "Oh, let me leave this earthly tabernacle, Lord!" I had prayed. "It has been long enough! I cannot go further by myself!"

But the Holy Spirit, my Comforter, held me up moment by moment and day by day for weeks and months, and now it was five years since my godmother had left me. The love and the pain in my heart were not less than on that day five years ago. The longing to join her before the Lord was no less intense. But then the sweet peace of Jesus, "which passeth all understanding" (Philippians 4:7), swept over me once more.

And I sang this song unto the Lord:
> Thy cross all my refuge, Thy blood all my plea,
> None other I need, blessed Jesus, but Thee!
> I fear not the shadows at close of life's day,
> For Thou wilt go with me the rest of the way!

A message came one day that Mrs. Billy Graham; the Grahams' youngest son, Ned; their daughter Bunny and her husband, Dr. Dienert, were coming to visit me. The Lord sustained me in my weakness and gave me unusual strength and quietness in my heart for this unexpected pleasure. As soon as we were introduced to each other, I prayed, asking the Lord Jesus to bless our fellowship for His glory. He did!

Mrs. Graham, who was born of missionary parents in China, told me she had read my book three times and that she was going to read it again. Strongly urging me to hurry and finish this sequel, she exclaimed, "Oh, Miss Tsai, you should stop all your meetings, keep people from coming to see you, and concentrate fully on finishing this witness! It will surely be used by the Lord to encourage many—even more than the meetings here in your dark chamber!"

I was led to ask her son-in-law to read the preface and the first chapter of this sequel. After he read it, he said, "This is what people want to read. They want to read actions of God's doings in a human being. Hurry and finish your sequel!"

In my human desire, this also would have been what I would have liked to do. But the Lord's call to me to be His "hunting dog" is still as clear as it was the day that I turned over my life to Him. "Mrs. Graham, you and I know that the coming of the Lord is near, even at the door!" I said. "If I refuse to see some person whose heart is prepared to accept Him, I would fail my Lord. I must be ready, by His help, to win people to Him and open the door into His sheepfold so that the lost sheep may find their way in. If it pleases the Lord that this little witness should be written, it must be done between the swinging of the doors while the lost sheep enter His fold and go 'in and out, and find pasture' " (John 10:9b).

Mrs. Graham kindly gave me permission to use this poem from her book:

> Test me, Lord, and give me strength
> to meet each test
>   unflinching, unafraid;
> not striving nervously to do my best,
> not self-assured, or careless as in jest,
>   but with Your aid.
>
> Purge me, Lord, and give me grace
> to bear the heat
>   of cleansing flame;
> not bitter at my lowly lot, but meet
> to bear my share of suffering and keep me sweet,
>   In Jesus' name.*

*From *Sitting By My Laughing Fire,* by Ruth Bell Graham, Copyright, 1977, Ruth Bell Graham, Word Books. Used by permission of Word Books, Publisher, Waco, Texas.

I keep a small magnet in my "miscellaneous drawer." Because of my poor eyesight and the darkened room, it is most difficult for me to rummage around to find exactly the tiny things that I want. I pull my magnet around, and all kinds of pins and objects jump to the magnet and cling there. It doesn't matter if they are crooked, bent, broken, small, or large. In 1 Thessalonians 4:17, believers are promised that at the coming of the Lord, we shall be "caught up . . . to meet the Lord in the air." In Chinese, the word translated "caught up" has the meaning of "pulled up" or "lifted up" like the action of a magnet. Not all the things in my drawer can be lifted up by my magnet—only those items which are magnetized. The other things just lie there with no response. So the Lord has reminded me that at His coming, whether new or old, bent, broken, or whatever—we who are His, and only those who are His—will be lifted up with Him.

Shall I only sit and wait for my King of light, my heavenly Bridegroom, to come and take me from the stage of my dark chamber so that my final curtain can come down? No! In His love and in His perfect plan revealed in His Word, He has said, "Occupy till I come" (Luke 19:13). So in spite of advanced age, infirmity, weakness, and increasing limitations, I joyously agree with Him that I must go on!

Dr. Oswald J. Smith has graciously allowed me to use his poem, "We Must Go On," which expresses my continued heart commitment to my Lord:

WE MUST GO ON

We must go on, the night is fast approaching,
The past is gone, we cannot change it now;
We weep, we pray, and yet forget we cannot,
O God, forgive, as at Thy Throne we bow.

We must go on, atone ourselves, we cannot,
Thy blood alone can make us clean within;
There is no hope except Thy love and mercy,
Then pardon, Lord, and take away our sin.

We must go on, the future still awaits us,
The present, too, is ours to live for Thee;
Our past, dear Lord, oh help us to forget it,
And by Thy power, come now and set us free.

We must go on, although our tears are falling,
For all our work on earth will soon be o'er;
Our prayers, our toils will someday be rewarded,
And we shall dwell with Thee forevermore.

We must go on, the Day will soon be dawning,
The future calls, we cannot change the past;
Thy plan is best and though our hearts are breaking,
We must go on, 'twill all be plain at last!

Moody Press, a ministry of the Moody Bible Institute, is
designed for education, evangelization, and edification.
If we may assist you in knowing more about Christ and
the Christian life, please write us without obligation:
Moody Press, c/o MLM, Chicago, Illinois 60610.